1 0 STEPS TO

Successful
Facilitation

PRESS

Alexandria, Virginia

ASTD Press is an internationally renowned source of insightful and practical information on workplace learning and performance topics, including training basics, evaluation and return-on-investment, instructional systems development, e-learning, leadership, and career development.

Ordering information: Books published by ASTD Press can be purchased by visiting our website at store.astd.org or by calling 800.628.2783 or 703.683.8100.

Library of Congress Control Number: 2008928375
ISBN-10: 1-56286-538-2
ISBN-13: 978-1-56286-538-2

ASTD Press Editorial Staff:
Director: Cat Russo
Manager, Acquisitions and Author Relations: Mark Morrow
Editorial Manager: Jacqueline Edlund-Braun
Senior Associate Editor: Tora Estep
Editorial Assistant: Maureen Soyars
Retail Trade Manager: Yelba Quinn
Writer: Lynn Lewis, Learning Solutions LLC
Copyeditor: Pamela Lankas
Indexer: Mary Kidd
Proofreader: IGS
Interior Design and Production: International Graphic Services
Cover Design: Kristi Sone

Printed by Victor Graphics, Inc., Baltimore, Maryland, www.victorgraphics.com

CONTENTS

Let's face it, most people spend their days in chaotic, fast-paced, time- and resource-strained organizations. Finding time for just one more project, assignment, or even learning opportunity—no matter how career enhancing or useful—is difficult to imagine. The *10 Steps* series is designed for today's busy professional who needs advice and guidance on a wide array of topics ranging from project management to people management, from business strategy to decision making and time management, from stepping in to deliver a presentation for someone else to researching and creating a compelling presentation as well as effectively delivering the content. Each book in this ASTD series promises to take its readers on a journey to basic understanding, with practical application the ultimate destination. This is truly a just-tell-me-what-to-do-now series. You will find action-driven language teamed with examples, worksheets, case studies, and tools to help you quickly implement the right steps and chart a path to your own success. The *10 Steps* series will appeal to a broad business audience from middle managers to upper-level management. Workplace learning and human resource professionals along with other professionals seeking to improve their value proposition in their organizations will find these books a great resource.

P R E F A C E

At one time or another, you've probably been part of a group charged with a mission-critical task and observed the group floundering ineffectively, barely able to get out of the starting blocks. Struggling to define their objectives, make decisions, and get procedures implemented, what the group needed was an effective facilitator.

A facilitator is a person who has no decision-making authority within a group but who guides the group to work together more efficiently, to create synergy, to generate new ideas, and to gain consensus and agreement. How do facilitators accomplish all of this? By helping to improve a group's processes—meaning the way the group works together, including how they talk to each other, identify and solve problems, make decisions, and handle conflict.

Facilitation skills are essential today for all professionals dealing with any kind of work groups including management, a board, top leadership, task forces, committees, project teams, and so on.

The thought of facilitating a meeting often ranks at the top of the list of what people fear the most. So how do you go about developing and facilitating an effective, results-oriented meeting? *10 Steps to Successful Facilitation* provides the key information you need to accomplish this goal. You can jump to any step in the 10-step process or start at the beginning. These steps include

1. understanding what facilitation is and knowing the audience
2. developing the facilitation plan
3. planning the facilitation content
4. using facilitation tools and techniques to engage participants
5. integrating media and technology for impact
6. preparing to facilitate
7. leveraging strategies to deal with group conflict and difficult participants
8. creating a climate for an effective facilitation session
9. facilitating with a business focus
10. evaluating how you did.

10 Steps to Successful Facilitation is part of the *10 Steps* series and was written to provide you with a proven process, quick reference tips, and practical worksheets to help you successfully facilitate any session or meeting. We hope that the tips and tools contained in this book will guide you each step of the way in developing and delivering an effective facilitation session.

INTRODUCTION

The art of facilitation involves processes and skills that help groups to function effectively. The fact is, facilitation is not about you—it is about the group. The purpose of facilitation is to guide a group to an agreed-upon destination or outcome. As such, facilitators often point participants in the right direction, make suggestions, take steps to enhance the experience for the participants, and give guidance—but do not do the work for the group.

Standing in the spotlight as the facilitator can be a scary and daunting experience. Successful facilitators leverage effective questioning techniques, elicit participation from group members, aid in generating ideas, and usher the group down a path to mutual agreement.

Because of the powerful nature of facilitation in accomplishing goals and objectives, today's business professionals are all expected to facilitate groups and processes at some point in time. It is therefore a necessary component of every professional's business acumen.

This book, *10 Steps to Successful Facilitation*, provides techniques for identifying the right participants to invite into the group and supplies the framework for developing an effective facilitation plan. Tips and examples given in each chapter help to guide you through the entire facilitation process from planning through facilitating and evaluating results.

Use the key steps in this book as needed. For example, if you have been asked to facilitate a meeting with a predefined agenda and plan, then you should perhaps focus on steps 4–10. Or, if you have been asked to facilitate a group for a new project in its infancy and you are faced with a completely blank slate, then it might be most appropriate to start with step 1 and work through all steps systematically.

This book focuses on
- defining facilitation and gathering information about the audience
- developing a facilitation plan
- planning a facilitation session
- using tools and techniques to engage the group
- integrating media and technology for impact
- tips and steps in preparing to facilitate a session or meeting
- defining the stages of group development and strategies for dealing with group conflict
- tools for creating an effective facilitation environment
- conducting the facilitation session and evaluating the meeting's success.

Structure of This Book

This book will help you to quickly identify the facilitation session goals and required participants, develop a facilitation plan, and effectively facilitate a session to help a group accomplish the defined goals and objectives. In particular, this book delves into each of the following steps:
- **Step 1: Get Started**—There are many myths regarding the role of a facilitator in helping a group achieve defined goals. For example, a facilitator is not a leader who directs

what the group should do. This chapter delves into defining facilitation; the differences between facilitators and presenters; roles of a facilitator; key facilitation processes; and how to identify the audience, group, or participants to involve.

- ◆ **Step 2: Develop the Facilitation Plan**—The goal of facilitation is to accomplish defined objectives. This chapter describes how to start the process by identifying the client's needs, the business goals, and objectives; determining if a meeting is appropriate; identifying who should participate; and preparing a meeting agenda.

- ◆ **Step 3: Plan a Facilitation Session**—With the groundwork laid, the next step involves developing a facilitation plan that outlines the content flow of the facilitation session, as well as questioning techniques, tools, and activities to engage participants.

- ◆ **Step 4: Use Facilitation Tools and Techniques to Engage Participants**—Effective groups do not just happen. Because a large percentage of a facilitator's time is spent helping groups to generate ideas and make decisions, this chapter describes a wealth of tools and activities that successful facilitators use to facilitate group problem solving and decision making.

- ◆ **Step 5: Integrate Media and Technology for Impact**—When facilitating a meeting, chances are that you'll need to leverage at least one type of media. This chapter describes the features and benefits of various types of media and visual aids to effectively facilitate sessions that clearly communicate information, capture ideas, and determine the best solutions.

- ◆ **Step 6: Prepare to Facilitate**—Successful facilitators understand that people learn and absorb in information in different ways. For that reason, successful facilitators cater to all of the different ways that group members prefer to take in and process information when preparing a facilitation session. This chapter describes different types of learning styles and preferences and how successful facilitators leverage various learning activities to accommodate the preferences of all group members.

◆ **Step 7: Leverage Strategies to Deal with Group Conflict and Difficult Participants**—At some point in your career, you will encounter combative or difficult participants who may be the "one bad apple to spoil the bunch." Or perhaps you have an entire group that is a bit dysfunctional and apathetically goes through the motions without making any progress toward accomplishing the group goals. This chapter delves into the stages of group development and the process of identifying and dealing with behaviors that enhance or hinder group effectiveness.

◆ **Step 8: Create an Effective Climate**—Staging the facilitation session environment can greatly affect facilitation success. No matter how well designed the facilitation plan, a good session in a poor environment can easily end up a waste of time for everyone involved. This chapter describes how to ensure that the physical setting of the room matches and enhances the facilitation session goals.

◆ **Step 9: Facilitate with a Business Focus**—Sweaty palms and butterflies can plague even the most seasoned facilitators, so what techniques do the pros use to combat nervousness and harness that energy and anxiety to work in their favor? This chapter provides ideas on how to get the facilitation session off to the right start, techniques for keeping facilitation sessions on track and for keeping discussions going, and best practices for communicating effectively. Being prepared is the best strategy to reduce anxiety and build confidence before beginning any facilitation session.

◆ **Step 10: Evaluate the Facilitation Session**—The last step in the facilitation process is to reflect back on the session and evaluate best practices or pitfalls. This important step ultimately leads to continuous improvement and refinement of your facilitation skills. This chapter identifies several strategies for obtaining and analyzing information to evaluate the session success.

Review these 10 steps as often as needed to build and perfect your ability to facilitate effective, performance-driven facilitation sessions.

Get Started

You've probably had a lot of experience participating or working in a group setting at one time or another. For many people, the experience is a mixed bag—at times, group members work well together and seem to almost share the same brain because their thoughts, ideas, and approaches on how to get something done are so similar. At other times the team flounders, inefficiently trying to muddle through coming up with basic goals and objectives, never coming to agreement, and eventually disbanding because of high levels of frustration. So what is a key component that often delineates successful groups from the inefficient? Facilitation.

What Is Facilitation?

Groups, a basic work unit of organizations, are often tasked with providing different views on a topic or issue, solving problems, coordinating complex work processes, and so on. Often these same work groups entrusted with creating mission-critical initiatives are ineffective and struggle to get decisions made and procedures implemented.

Enter facilitation. A facilitator is a person who has no decision-making authority within a group but who guides the group to work more efficiently together, to create synergy, to generate new ideas, and to gain consensus and agreement. How do facilitators accomplish all of this? By helping to improve a group's processes—meaning how the group works together, including how they talk to each other, identify and solve problems, make decisions, and handle conflict.

Facilitation skills are essential today for all professionals dealing with any kind of work groups including management, executive boards, top leadership, task forces, committees, project teams, and so on.

Facilitators come from many different backgrounds and may hold various roles within or external to an organization, such as leaders, managers, consultants, coaches, trainers, and formal facilitators.

Facilitation skills apply to you whether or not you are a facilitator. The fact is, facilitation skills are assumed to be part of every professional's business acumen in today's work environment. So how do you develop these skills? With knowledge and practice.

It's Not About You

One of the key tenets of facilitation is that the process and experience is not about you—it is about the participants. The purpose of facilitation is to guide a group to an agreed-upon destination or outcome. As such, facilitators often point participants in the right direction, make suggestions, take steps to enhance the experience for the participants, and offer guidance—but do not do the work for group.

What's the Difference Between a Facilitator and a Presenter?

Facilitators are usually individuals who assist teams in their meetings to enhance the process—how the team works and comes to decisions. Generally, the facilitator is not involved in the process or task being examined: He or she is not a stakeholder and may begin team involvement knowing nothing about what is being discussed. Good facilitators ensure that teams don't get too bogged down in personality or process issues and that every individual within the group is heard.

A facilitator's role often includes

- coaching the team in process, roles, procedures, policies, and goals
- attending team meetings on an as-needed basis to provide feedback to the team leader and members
- acting as a regular consultant to the team leader
- monitoring team dynamics, diagnosing problems, and managing appropriate interventions
- promoting the team concept.

POINTER Identify the purpose and expectations of the facilitator's role before taking on the task. A facilitator is not a "leader" who leads a group and makes decisions. Rather, the facilitator enables the group to identify problems, generate ideas, and decide on the best solution.

Effective facilitators are responsible and accountable to the group; therefore, the facilitator's role is one of earned trust and honor. It's a different role from a teacher/instructor/presenter in a classroom, where there is a clear and obvious separation between the learners and the presenter, and in which the presenter is positioned as an expert who knows all. In that situation, the learners are merely passive recipients of the knowledge.

Three main characteristics differentiate facilitators from presenters: focus, control, and credibility.

- **Focus:** A facilitator focuses on the participants, whereas a presenter focuses on self and the content.

POINTER

Identify the business goals and objectives of the facilitation session. If a clear purpose for the meeting or facilitation session is not provided, beware! Identify at least one or two outcomes—so that even if no other issues are addressed, the meeting is still deemed a success.

◆ **Control:** A facilitator shares control of the session and the environment with the participants, but a presenter controls all facets.

◆ **Credibility:** A facilitator derives credibility from using presentation, interpersonal, and questioning skills; managing the environment; sharing ideas; remaining flexible; and driving the group to agreement, whereas a presenter derives credibility solely from demonstrating subject matter expertise and presentation skills.

Roles of a Facilitator

Facilitators wear many hats during the course of a meeting—all of which are critical to creating an effective experience. No matter which hats or tasks you take on as a facilitator, it is imperative that you remain neutral when guiding the group through its process stages. Skilled facilitators strive for excellence in three main areas: managing the facilitation process, acting as a resource, and remaining neutral.

Managing the Process

Managing the facilitation process includes
- striving for consensus
- keeping members on task
- following the agenda
- focusing on problem solving
- controlling the flow of contributions
- rewarding and motivating group members.

Acting as a Resource

The facilitator acts as a resource to the group. This involves

- advising on problem-solving methods
- providing on-the-spot training in group process techniques
- protecting group members from personal attacks.

Remaining Neutral

It is essential that the facilitator remain neutral. This involves

- staying emotionally uninvolved
- keeping out of the spotlight
- becoming invisible when the group is facilitating itself
- keeping silent on content issues.

Required Skills

The facilitator's role, while rather broad, is crucial to the success of the team. A good facilitator basically checks his or her personal concerns and causes at the door. The most successful facilitators excel in the following areas:

- **Listening**—a facilitator needs to be able to listen actively and hear what every team member is saying.
- **Questioning**—a facilitator should be skilled in asking questions. Good questions are open-ended and stimulate discussion.
- **Sharing**—a facilitator should be able to share his or her feelings and create an atmosphere in which group members are willing to share their feelings and opinions.

POINTER

Determine if a meeting is truly necessary or if there is a better alternative. If the purpose of the meeting is only to communicate information, then it may be more efficient to provide the information in writing and distribute it electronically.

Plan on doing some advance work. Most meetings involve some prework or homework on the part of the participants. Plan appropriate premeeting activities for participants such as reading documents or researching information to make the most effective use of the facilitation session time.

- **Problem Solving**—facilitators should be skilled at applying group problem-solving techniques and processes including
  - defining the problem
  - determining the cause
  - considering alternatives
  - weighing the alternatives
  - selecting the best alternative
  - implementing the solution
  - evaluating the results.
- **Resolving Conflict**—conflict among group members should not be suppressed. Indeed, it should be expected and dealt with constructively. This includes barring personal attacks.
- **Using a Participative Style**—a facilitator should be able to encourage all team members to actively engage and participate in meetings.
- **Being Accepting of Others**—a facilitator should maintain an open mind and not criticize the ideas and suggestions of group members.
- **Empathizing**—a facilitator should be able to "walk a mile in another's shoes" to understand the team members' feelings, and he or she should be able to express these feelings.
- **Leading**—a facilitator must be able to keep participants focused and the discussion on target.

Creating an Audience Profile

In an ideal situation, you have all the information you need about your audience before you begin facilitating a meeting so you can plan which techniques and activities will engage participants and achieve the desired outcomes. To aid in this process, successful facilitators gather as much information as possible about the goal of the facilitation session as well as the audience.

To achieve these results, facilitators spend time researching

- the skill and background levels of the participants
- job context information, including whether the participants work alone or in groups; levels of activity and movement they are accustomed to; and where they are in their work cycle when they attend the facilitation session (for example, are they just ending the graveyard shift and showing up for the session exhausted?).
- the learning styles and preferences of participants and what they are or are not accustomed to
- the level of flexibility, openness to change, and willingness to share opinions or try new ways of doing things
- the participants' attitudes toward the topic(s) to be discussed
- circumstances leading to their participation (is it mandatory or voluntary).

POINTER

If possible, select the time of day for the facilitation session. For example, if the meeting is expected to take several hours or half of a day—perhaps schedule the facilitation session in the morning when everyone is awake and more energetic rather than late in the afternoon.

Taking time to gather this information prior to the facilitation session will help arm you with the key information required to structure the meeting and to appropriately plan how many and what types of activities might be most effective to achieve the desired outcomes.

If you do not have time prior to the facilitation session to identify this information about the participants, plan some contingency activities such as an opening or warm-up activity to gather this information at the start of the session.

Now that you have an appreciation of what a facilitator does and the responsibilities that accompany the role, use Worksheet 1.1 to evaluate your effectiveness and identify areas in which you can enhance your skills.

The next step in the process involves working with the client or primary contact to clarify the business objectives, to clarify the goals for the facilitation session, to determine the expectations of the facilitator, and to create an initial agenda.

WORKSHEET 1.1
Facilitator Self-Assessment Role Inventory

Use this self-assessment to reflect on your effectiveness regarding the various roles of a facilitator and to evaluate areas for improvement. Below are statements regarding the role of the facilitator. Using the scale provided, indicate the extent to which you fulfill that particular role. For areas rated 2 or below, identify specific actions you plan to take to improve in that area.

0 = not at all
1 = to a very little extent
2 = to a little or some extent
3 = to a great extent
4 = to a very great extent

	ROLE	RATING					ACTIONS
		1	2	3	4	5	
1.	Creates and sustains an environment conducive for discussions and idea generation.	❏	❏	❏	❏	❏	
2.	Develops group cohesiveness.	❏	❏	❏	❏	❏	
3.	Manages group-involvement processes.	❏	❏	❏	❏	❏	
4.	Promotes the development of action and follow-up plans.	❏	❏	❏	❏	❏	
5.	Establishes timing as a ground rule.	❏	❏	❏	❏	❏	
6.	Starts sessions on time.	❏	❏	❏	❏	❏	
7.	Manages the time to ensure all agenda topics are covered in the allotted time.	❏	❏	❏	❏	❏	
8.	Stops on time.	❏	❏	❏	❏	❏	
9.	Asks in-depth questions.	❏	❏	❏	❏	❏	

(continued on next page)

ROLE	RATING 1	2	3	4	5	ACTIONS
10. Uses a variety of questioning techniques and types to generate discussion and facilitate a deeper level of thinking.	❐	❐	❐	❐	❐	
11. Shares experiences that enhance credibility.	❐	❐	❐	❐	❐	
12. Uses appropriate jargon for the topic and participants.	❐	❐	❐	❐	❐	
13. Maintains a positive, professional demeanor.	❐	❐	❐	❐	❐	
14. Helps participants to understand key concepts as they relate to the topics being discussed.	❐	❐	❐	❐	❐	
15. Helps others to identify problems.	❐	❐	❐	❐	❐	
16. Intervenes appropriately when things go wrong.	❐	❐	❐	❐	❐	
17. Uses a systematic approach.	❐	❐	❐	❐	❐	
18. Uses time efficiently.	❐	❐	❐	❐	❐	
19. Listens actively.	❐	❐	❐	❐	❐	
20. Deals constructively with disruptive behaviors.	❐	❐	❐	❐	❐	
21. Shares objectives with the group.	❐	❐	❐	❐	❐	

Develop the Facilitation Plan

Understanding the client's
needs

Identifying business goals
and objectives

Determining if a meeting
is needed

Who should participate

Planning effective
facilitation sessions

Preparing an agenda

People often have multiple roles in a meeting. If you were to look at a spectrum of roles from meeting or logistics planner to organizational development consultant, the role of facilitator would probably fall somewhere in the middle.

Facilitators are responsible for assessing the needs of the group, planning and structuring the best activities, using tools and techniques to accomplish the desired outcomes, and setting up meeting logistics. Once information is known about the group, the next step involves digging into details with the client or primary contact to create a facilitation plan.

Understanding the Client's Needs

When an opportunity to facilitate a meeting arises, you should spend some upfront discovery time to gather information and confirm that the need for facilitation exists.

Sometimes groups need a facilitator to help solve a problem with how the group is currently functioning, to help manage conflict, or to introduce tools and techniques for idea generation and problem solving.

No matter what business need gave rise to the opportunity, an initial conversation with your client or primary contact is essential. During this conversation, you should explore the client's motivation, previous experience with facilitators, and the business goals and objectives.

The purpose of this meeting is not to diagnose all of the group's problems; rather, it is to gain insight into the client's goals, interests, and concerns. This is also an excellent time to help set expectations regarding your approach to facilitation, to identify whether the group has already agreed to any decisions, and to gain agreement on the next steps in the process.

Identifying the Business Goals and Objectives

An effectively facilitated meeting begins with a purpose. You have a good reason for calling the meeting, you carefully plan its execution, and continually guide the group with that purpose in mind. Every decision you make—from whom to invite to how to run it— revolves around the meeting's goal.

After the client meeting, when you understand the scope of the initiative and can confirm that facilitation is appropriate, the next step is to define the specific purpose for the meeting. Drafting the business goals and objectives not only clarifies your role but also helps to ensure that the client and you are both on the same page.

When crafting the meeting or initiative objectives, evaluate them by thinking SMART: Are they **s**pecific, **m**easurable, **a**chievable, **r**ealistic, and **t**imebound? What outcomes would indicate that the group achieved the meeting objective?

Outcomes define the tangible end products of a meeting or initiative. What do the client and you want as a result of the meeting: an agreed-upon decision? A recommendation? A prioritized list of ideas?

A clearly defined outcome statement is a product—not a process. It should focus on nouns to describe the end result (for example, lists, timelines, solutions to a problem) and on a set of realistic goals that can be accomplished within the time constraints of the meeting. Producing a detailed project plan for a new initiative probably is not realistic for a two-hour meeting. For example, a meeting objective might be to determine the causes behind the declining sales of X product and to identify at least three viable solutions to the problem. So, having the group brainstorm or generate at least three viable solutions is the stated outcome, indicating success for the meeting.

Determining If a Meeting Is Appropriate

At this point in the process, it is important to determine if a facilitated meeting is really the best use of everyone's time to meet the client's goals and objectives. Facilitated meetings are most appropriate and effective when

POINTER Facilitators are experts in the process of facilitation—not necessarily the content being discussed or decided on during the meeting.

- ◆ the goal is to present information to a group of people quickly and to gather input or to gain buy-in
- ◆ you can state the business goals and objectives for the meeting
- ◆ the meeting purpose is worth the time and cost of calling in participants
- ◆ a meeting is going to be a more efficient and accurate way to convey information than sending an email or making phone calls

- you plan to act on people's input
- the participants and you have enough time to adequately prepare for the meeting
- the participants are going to be able to work together on the issue or problem.

Although you may have more than one purpose for calling a meeting, be careful not to pack in too much. Information or activity overload—giving too much news at one time or asking people to solve too many problems at once—destroys meeting effectiveness.

Whatever the goal or purpose of the facilitation session, be sure to explain it in advance. Attendees should know ahead of time, for instance, whether they're present to listen to a report or to help solve a problem. Sharing the expectations for attendee participation not only helps to set expectations, but also satisfies their curiosity and helps them to adequately prepare for the meeting.

Determining Who Should Participate

People's time is a valuable resource both in terms of what it costs and what else they can achieve in that time. For that reason, you need to ensure that the people asked to participate in the meeting are those most likely to contribute and help to achieve the desired business outcomes.

Another reason to be selective is that with each new person, group dynamics grow more complex, and achieving meeting objectives becomes trickier. Be choosy about the participants to invite. To help make this decision, answer the following questions and articulate a reason for each person to attend:

- Who needs the information you are going to share? Who needs the information firsthand?
- From whom do you need to get firsthand information?

Characteristics of Effective Meetings

No matter what the purpose, all productive meetings share similar characteristics. Use these hints to get a successful facilitation session off the ground:

- All participants have a valid reason for being included in the meeting.
- All participants know the purpose of the meeting and arrive prepared to fulfill that purpose.
- The meeting is as brief as possible and sticks to the agenda.
- Objectives, also called desired outcomes, determined in advance, are achieved by the end of the meeting.
- All parties leave the meeting knowing what was accomplished and what is expected of them in the future.

Some conditions that must also exist to help drive a successful meeting include:

- The meeting has a specified leader (normally the person who called the meeting). A facilitator helps to guide the group—he or she does not impose answers or authority.
- Participants understand their roles, respect the other participants, and feel responsible for the meeting content and outcomes.
- The meeting atmosphere is safe and supportive— participants feel free to express their views frankly, without fear of repercussion.
- Participants display interest in and respect for others' viewpoints.

- Who is directly affected by the problem?
- Who can contribute to the achievement of the meeting objectives?
- Who has the authority to approve of a solution or take action?
- Should the participants included in the meeting represent different organizational levels? In general, meetings work best with participants of equal status; they are more relaxed, so discussions are more open and productive.
- Should each department or division be represented?
- Should anyone be invited purely for political reasons?

If the meeting's purpose is to discuss a controversial issue, make sure you invite an equal number of participants from both sides of the issue. And make sure that both sides of the issue are represented by people of equal status.

POINTER

A facilitator should always be neutral and objective. The mark of a successful facilitator is that participants feel that they have done the work themselves—and have not been influenced by the facilitator's views and opinions.

Be sure to consider the number of participants on your list. Is it a manageable group in view of the objectives you need to accomplish? If, for example, the only objective is to have participants hear about a new policy, you can achieve that objective with a large group. If, however, there is another objective such as brainstorming ways of applying the new policy for profit, a shorter list of participants will be more effective when conducting the brainstorming segment. Usually groups no larger than 10 are best for decision-making and problem-solving sessions.

After identifying the participants, the next step involves determining what you

Meeting Roles

Facilitators conduct productive meetings in an efficient, smooth manner and document the results for follow-up actions. To accomplish this, the most successful facilitators may enlist participants to function as timekeeper, facilitator, and note-taker. In the event of recurring meetings, such as a weekly project-status meeting, perhaps assign the roles to a different person each session.

Timekeeper

- Effective meetings start and end on time. To help make that happen, use a timekeeper. The timekeeper notes the amount of time allotted on the agenda for each activity and keeps track of the actual amount of time spent. If the group goes beyond the allotted time for an activity, the timekeeper interrupts (gently) and asks the group to make a decision: Should they continue the activity now or at a later meeting? If a discussion is particularly productive, moving other agenda items to another meeting can be worthwhile, but first gain agreement from participants.

Facilitator

- Facilitation is a highly desirable skill set that requires learning and practice. People often underestimate its importance and difficulty. During a meeting, the facilitator has two main jobs: to draw out quiet participants and to prevent other participants from dominating the discussion. To draw out quiet participants, consider
  - asking by name if the person has anything to contribute
  - recognizing when someone has made a contribution
  - asking a question and having everyone respond to it at one time. (continued on next page)

A slightly sneaky way to keep someone from dominating the discussion is to assign that person the role of the facilitator. Other ways include interrupting gently and asking someone else for his or her opinions or reminding everyone of the time limits on agenda items.

Note-taker

The note-taker serves as the official historian for the meeting. Depending on the structure of the meeting, he or she might take notes on a flipchart and periodically confirm with the group that points are recorded accurately. Alternatively, the note-taker may keep notes on a pad of paper or electronically, use an electronic whiteboard, and so on. No matter how notes are captured during the session, as a best practice, they should always be typed up and distributed to all participants.

With an audience profile in hand, the next step in becoming a successful facilitator is to develop the facilitation plan, including determining the business drivers that gave rise to the facilitation need, the goals, and the objectives; identifying the participants to include; and planning for the kickoff and subsequent meetings.

need to know about each person to accomplish the stated objectives as well as to identify what each person's responsibilities for the meeting will be. For example, do you need

- ◆ to know in advance whether each participant has experience with the type of project to be discussed
- ◆ what each person's expectations are concerning the initiative
- ◆ someone to provide specific background information

- someone else to come prepared with suggestions and ideas for discussion
- the participants to read a report and be able to discuss it intelligently?

You also need to determine if you need everyone to attend the entire meeting or only part of it.

Another type of responsibility that you may require of participants is for them to play specific meeting roles such as timekeeper, facilitator, and note-taker. Whatever you ask of your participants, make sure that you give them a sufficient amount of time to prepare. How many times have you been in a meeting and found that you have information relevant to the topic, but you weren't asked to bring it, or to review it in advance?

Planning Effective Facilitation Sessions

No matter what the purpose, all productive meetings share similar characteristics. Responsibility for these characteristics and conditions is shared by the facilitator and by the participants. To help get your facilitation session off to the right start, focus on these characteristics:

- All participants have a valid reason for being included in the meeting.

POINTER

When estimating how long a facilitation session should take, guesstimate how much time each agenda item will need and document it on the agenda. These estimates provide the group and you with benchmarks on which to gauge the pace of the meeting, to help keep the meeting on track, and suggest the need for prompts if timing adjustments need to occur.

POINTER

Consider sequencing the agenda with the most important items first. The exceptions to this rule include when you need to logically sequence topics to lead participants down a path to understand all issues and topics or when it is helpful to give a quick status update or get administrative tasks out of the way.

◆ All participants know the purpose of the meeting and arrive prepared to fulfill that purpose.
◆ The meeting is as brief as possible and sticks to the agenda.
◆ Objectives, or desired outcomes, are determined in advance and are achieved by the end of the meeting.
◆ All parties leave the meeting knowing what was accomplished and what is expected of them in the future.

After answering these questions and determining what you need to know, the next step is to create an agenda and outline based on the objectives.

Preparing a Meeting Agenda

A meeting agenda lists the topics and the order in which they will be covered. When sequencing the meeting topics try to structure the topics logically, always keeping the purpose of the meeting in mind. When creating the agenda, consider these points:

◆ Cover the topics in order of importance, with the most important topic first. Doing so takes advantage of early-meeting energy and guarantees full coverage of the most important topics.
◆ Some experts recommend the reverse—that is, covering the least important topic first and building to the most important topic. This technique enables participants to warm up and get minor matters out of the way.

- If one topic naturally leads to another, a sequence of topics in a logical order often works best.
- Try to end the agenda on a positive note—introduce something about which you expect to gain general approval from participants.
- Fill in activities planned to cover each topic. For example, the activities for one topic may be group discussion and debate, whereas the activities for another may be stating an identified problem and brainstorming solutions.
- Fill in how much time you expect each activity to take. Allow enough time for full participation by meeting attendees.

After creating an agenda that lists the flow of all topics and activities that you'll need to pursue to accomplish the session objectives, you need to assign realistic timeframes for each activity. The time estimates serve as a barometer for the pace of the meeting and accomplishing all objectives.

Finalizing the meeting agenda will not only help you to keep the meeting on track, but it will also be useful when you evaluate the success of the session and whether defined goals were accomplished. As a best practice, send the agenda to participants along with the meeting invitation. This enables them to review the topics to be covered and helps them prepare in advance.

POINTER

When planning the facilitation session agenda, be as specific as possible. Each agenda item should be geared to accomplishing the business goal or objective of the meeting. If it is not, then consider if it really belongs on the agenda.

Worksheet 2.1 will help you keep track of all that is required to plan a successful facilitation session so you can focus on specifics and maximize your meeting's effectiveness.

WORKSHEET 2.1
Planning a Facilitation Session

When planning a facilitation session, use this worksheet as a guide to verify that a meeting is appropriate, to identify the appropriate participants to attend, to assign who needs to do what, to identify basic equipment needs, and to capture the meeting goals and objectives.

Is a Meeting Necessary?

Answer the following questions to determine if a meeting is the best option.

Question	Yes or No?
Can you clearly state the purpose of the meeting?	
Do you need to solicit input from others to solve a problem, plan a project, or brainstorm?	
Do you need to deliver information to a lot of people but don't want to write it?	
Do you want to motivate and energize a group or team?	

If you answered "no" to any of these questions—stop here. You probably do not need a meeting or facilitation session. Consider making phone calls, or sending an email or memo instead. If you do need to call a meeting, confirm the purpose here: _____

Identifying the Right Participants

Considering what needs to be achieved, who can make contributions to the goals and success of the meeting? Who needs to come? List the names of the people you are considering and then note the reason that person should come. If you can't think of a good reason for someone to attend, then you should probably remove his or her name from the list. For optimum efficiency, keep in mind that larger groups have more complex dynamics and are more difficult to manage. Determine the appropriate number of people to attend based on the topics and type of facilitation session planned.

Name	Reason to Attend?

Who Needs to Do What?

Now that you've decided whom to invite, determine if you need someone to carry out any specific tasks in the session, such as presenting information or coming up with some preliminary ideas. Also identify who you want to carry out the roles of timekeeper, facilitator, and note-taker.

Task or Role	Name
Timekeeper	
Facilitator	
Note-taker	

What Type of Meeting Location and Equipment Are Needed?

To identify the facilities and equipment needed, consider the following questions:

◆ Do you have a space that is big enough to comfortably accommodate all participants?

◆ Do you need any special seating arrangements?

◆ Is the meeting going to take long enough to require breaks or refreshments?

◆ How are you planning to facilitate the session? Who will take notes?

◆ Is the equipment that you need available in the room or facilities you have chosen?

What Needs to Get Done?

The last component in planning a meeting is determining what's going to happen. To identify the right agenda items in the right quantity, answer these questions.

◆ What has to happen to accomplish the session objectives?

◆ What is the most important outcome from the meeting?

◆ If the meeting were cut in half for some reason, what would be the first item removed from the agenda?

◆ If this is a follow-up meeting, were agenda items left from the last meeting that should be taken care of?

◆ During which activity are meeting participants going to commit to further action and next steps?

◆ Are there any minor issues that could be quickly cleared up during this meeting?

Now list the agenda topics and activities. Mark each activity as high (H) or low (L) priority. You may want to keep low-priority activities on the agenda and remove them if time constraints require you to focus on other topics. If possible, facilitate the high-priority activities first both to capitalize on the energy of the group and to ensure that you cover them.

Topics	Activities	Priority (H/L)

Plan the Facilitation Session

OVERVIEW

Developing a strong opening

Establishing the purpose, outcomes, and agenda

Choosing the right techniques to accomplish session goals

With the groundwork laid, the next step in the process is to plan the content flow and choose the tools and activities you will use to guide the facilitation session.

Most successful facilitators create a detailed outline that lists all activities that will take place during the meeting. They keep selected activities focused on achieving the stated objectives and prioritize them in terms of importance.

When planning the flow of discussion and activities, as a best practice, focus on your most important tasks first, unless you have one or two minor items to quickly clear off the list.

The outline should detail the estimated amount of time that the activities should take and indicate who is responsible for each activity. For some activities, it may be helpful to describe the process you plan to use when completing activities.

As a guideline, the outline should be complete enough that the meeting could run without you. You won't be able to harness the full effectiveness of the participants if they don't know what is expected of them. However, you shouldn't be married to the agenda either. If the discussion is productive, and the time allotted for that activity has elapsed, don't be afraid to ask the participants if they want to continue with the discussion and meet again to go over the remaining agenda.

Successful facilitation session outlines often include the following components:

Anticipate conflicting views, problems, and challenges. Successful facilitators not only spend time anticipating the differing views and issues that may come up during a facilitation session, but they actively plan which facilitation tools and techniques will be most effective to combat these challenges.

- **Strong opening**—which may include using icebreakers, reviewing the agenda, clarifying the purpose and objectives, establishing ground rules, and explaining the purpose of the parking lot.
- **Tasks to be completed**—which can be facilitated with guided discussions, questioning techniques, transitions, stories, action planning, debriefing sessions, and so on.
- **Effective closing**—which often summarizes the key points and confirms responsibilities for action items and next steps.

This chapter will explore all of the components to consider when planning a facilitation session and developing a detailed meeting outline.

Developing a Strong Opening

How often have you attended a meeting that quickly fell flat after the housekeeping details were discussed? This would not have happened if the facilitator had used an icebreaker! Icebreakers include several types of activities such as openers, warm-up exercises, and acquainters. These activities immediately get people involved, foster interaction, stimulate creative thinking, challenge basic assumptions, illustrate new concepts, and introduce specific material.

- **Openers and warm-ups**—these icebreakers warm up a group by stimulating, challenging, and motivating the participants. They can be used to begin a session, start a discussion, prime the group after a break, or to shift the topic focus.
- **Acquainters**—these icebreakers serve two functions: 1) they establish nonthreatening introductory contacts, and 2) they increase participants' familiarity with one another and usually are not tied to the meeting content directly.

Openers

Openers differ from acquainters in that they introduce or tie in to the topic of the facilitation session. They are intended to set the stage, avoid abrupt starts, and generally make participants comfortable with the facilitation session they are about to experience. They may energize groups after coffee breaks or lunch and may be used to open subsequent meetings in the facilitation process.

An effective opening is crucial to the start of any meeting because it bridges from whatever the audience members were doing before the meeting to the purpose of the meeting, the agenda, and tasks to achieve.

The opening of a facilitation session should not only help to establish the credibility of the facilitator, but should also accomplish three things:

- grab the participants' attention
- express the main goal of the meeting
- detail the benefit and explain what the audience can expect to get out of the facilitation session.

How to Use Icebreakers

This section provides some ideas of openers and how they can be used in facilitation sessions. You may need to personalize these ideas so that they are applicable to the session content and objectives.

For small-group facilitated meetings, ask participants to introduce themselves. Sharing names, roles, and relevant background information will not only help the group to get acquainted and become comfortable with each other for that session, but will be important if the group continues to work together in subsequent meetings over a period of time.

Acquainters

Acquainters may have no relation to the topic of the presentation. They are designed to put participants at ease and relieve the initial anxiety that comes with any new beginning.

How to Use

Personalize these acquainters to apply to your presentations:

- ◆ **Fancy Sayings**—this activity challenges the audience to "translate" written communications. For example, project the following on a screen and have them "decode" the meaning.
  - ◆ A feathered vertebrate enclosed in the grasping organ has an estimated worth that is higher than a duo encapsulated in the branched shrub. (A bird in the hand is worth two in the bush.)
  - ◆ It is sufficiently more tolerable to bestow upon than to come into possession. (It is better to give than to receive.)

- The medium of exchange is the origin or source of the amount of sorrow, distress, and calamity. (Money is the root of all evil.)
- A monetary unit equal to 1/100 of a pound that is stored aside is a monetary unit equal to 1/100 of a pound that is brought in by way of returns. (A penny saved is a penny earned.)

Openings should both explain the topic of the meeting and capture the audience's attention. Do not attempt the second without covering the first. Remember, if your attention-grabber does not tie into the topic, you will only confuse and distract the audience. Some best practices for openings follow:

- State the purpose or goal of the facilitation session. All participants will want to know why they are there and what is expected of them early in the process.
- Make the opening relevant to real-life experiences. This helps participants grasp the topic of the facilitation session by relating it to something they understand.
- Ask questions to stimulate thinking on the meeting topic. Besides stimulating the thought process, this technique helps participants to focus on the topic. These might be rhetorical questions or a show of hands.
- Share a personal experience or anecdote that is universal. You will spark participant interest if they have experienced something similar. But limit your "war" stories; too many can turn off interest.
- Give a unique demonstration. This works well with technical topics. You can then proceed from the introduction to explanations of the "why" and "how" of the demonstration.

(continued on next page)

> ◆ Use an interesting or famous quotation, or perhaps turn this quotation around just a bit to fit the topic. For example: "Ask not what work teams can do for you, but what you can do for your work team."
>
> ◆ Relate the topic to previously covered content. Perhaps the speaker who preceded you has established the groundwork for your presentation topic.

Acquainters

Acquainters need not have any direct tie to the facilitation session. They are designed to put group members at ease and relieve the initial anxiety that comes with any new situation.

Establishing the Purpose, Outcomes, Agenda, and the Parking Lot

The other key components of successful facilitation sessions should help the participants to clearly understand the goal of the session, what the task is, why they are doing it, and the desired outcome at the end of the facilitation session. These are accomplished by communicating the purpose and outcomes, as well as by reviewing the agenda.

The most successful facilitators usually provide a handout or display a flipchart detailing the agenda and estimated timing. This is an excellent point in the process to explain the goals of the session and the planned approach to achieve the meeting outcomes. This is also the ideal time to provide clarification on any points to participants. Be sure to check for their understanding and agreement. Often participants may want to modify or add to the outlined topics, approach, or process. Try to gain group consensus and buy-in because it is really the group that will be performing the work and achieving the goals—remember, as a facilitator you are a guide on the journey.

Establishing Ground Rules

Ground rules are behavioral expectations that facilitators and participants have of each other to support the group's efforts. Developing ground rules can be an excellent opening activity. Depending on your assessment of which activity will work best, you can

- present a list of proposed ground rules and facilitate an activity in which the participants react to and revise them
- facilitate an activity in which the participants propose their own ground rules and then come to consensus or vote on them.

The best way to get buy-in is to have the group define its own ground rules for the meeting. If you feel that the group has overlooked an area that should be addressed such as confidentiality, ask them to consider what is needed and decide how they would like to handle it.

When the group establishes and agrees to the ground rules, post them so that they are always visible. Quite often groups will "self-police" themselves, which means participants call each other on the ground rules when one is broken. Depending on the formality of the environment, the "calling" method can be as low key as the participants simply committing

POINTER

Clarify the group's responsibility. As a facilitator, you enable the group to accomplish the stated goals and objectives. Make it clear to the group that your role is to help them identify issues, generate ideas, and decide on the best course of action—however, it is their responsibility to do the work. The group needs to clearly understand their responsibility and feel empowered to make decisions so they can actively engage in the process.

STEP **3**

POINTER

Tips for Creating Ground Rules

It is best to write out ground rules and display them every time the group meets. Don't short change this process! The upfront time spent is well worth the investment because the burden of policing the group often transfers from the facilitator to the group. Not only does this help to keep discussions on track with the agenda, but it also promotes and maintains friendly group relations. To help you get started, consider using some of these ground rules for your facilitation sessions:

- Meetings begin and end on time.
- Attendees must actively participate.
- Turn off cell phones, PDAs, or any distractors.
- One person talks at a time.
- No side conversations are permitted.
- Respect others and their opinions, even if different from yours.
- Speak up if you have something to say.
- What is said in this room is confidential and stays within the group.
- The group needs to come to consensus when making decisions. If necessary, the group will vote to come to agreement.

to point it out verbally, all the way to verbalizing a key word, and throwing paper wads or Nerf balls at the offender.

Creating a Parking Lot

One tool used by successful facilitators is the parking lot. This tool establishes a designated place to collect ideas or topics that are off the agenda. These ideas may be more relevant to subsequent meetings or may have value that the group decides to visit at a later date. By documenting these items in the parking lot, the partici-pants can "let go of any baggage" to focus on the current topics and tasks and acknowledge any ideas or questions that need to be addressed at a later date. Placing items in the parking lot enables the group to keep moving forward while avoiding tangents that sidetrack the group's progress. Parking lot items should be docu-mented and revisited at the end of the session. The group should determine if the parking lot items should be included in future meeting agendas or if any action is required by group participants outside of meetings.

Transitions

Transitions help you move from point to point in a smooth, flow-ing manner. They are segues to the different parts of your meeting outline and are important in making the facilitation session cohe-sive and understandable. For example, once the group appears to have reached consensus on a topic, check for agreement from the group: "So are we all in agreement? Jack, did we address your con-cerns? Is everyone okay with the definitions and tasks we defined for these job roles?"

Choosing the Right Facilitation Techniques to Accomplish Session Goals

After planning the facilitation session opening, the next step in de-veloping the meeting outline is to plan the activities that will help guide the group in completing the stated tasks to achieve the de-sired outcomes. For example, an outcome might be for the group to create a list of 10 suggestions to assess the current morale of a par-ticular department. As you are designing the meeting outline, se-lect the most appropriate tool or technique to lead to the desired outcome.

Successful facilitators leverage a variety of facilitation tech-niques and understand *when* to use a particular technique as much as *how* to use it. Some basic facilitation techniques include

◆ **Listening**—if you expect the group members to actively participate, then you need to be sure to listen to what they are saying. After posing a question, pause and give them time to think and formulate their responses. When someone begins to respond, avoid assuming that you know what he or she is going to say. Nothing dampens a group's discussions faster than a facilitator who interrupts or jumps to hasty conclusions about a particular point— which may be incorrect. Pose a question, give the audience time to think, and then truly listen to participant input. Let the group drive the discussions—your role is to guide them to help achieve the stated outcomes.

◆ **Accepting different opinions and views**—if you are asking for ideas, comments, and thoughts on a topic, then be prepared for views that differ from yours. If you don't agree with something, be sure that you do not leave the audience with the impression that you agree or that the information is correct if it is not. If answers to questions aren't quite on target, then redirect the question and open it up to others by asking, "What do the rest of you think?"

◆ **Silence**—silence is an effective facilitation technique and one that novice facilitators often struggle with the most. Pausing enables the group to process what you are saying and to form their own thoughts and opinions.

This next section delves into additional facilitation techniques to get discussions going. These include questioning techniques as well as guided discussion, storytelling, humor, quotations, metaphors, analogies, anecdotes, communicating data, use of tables and graphs, action planning, and debriefing sessions.

Questioning Techniques

This is probably the most common way to encourage participation from a group—and is a skill that serves business professionals both inside and outside of a meeting room. There are several types of questions including open-ended, close-ended, hypothetical, and rhetorical. The ability to ask strong questions requires skill, practice, and planning.

Open-Ended Questions

Open-ended questions usually require participants to respond using more than one word—thereby expressing their thoughts, ideas, feelings, and opinions.

POINTER

Send facilitation session logistics information to participants in advance, including the date and time of the meeting, the meeting location, and any work that needs to be completed in advance of the meeting.

For example:

◆ "With a show of hands, how many of you currently spend at least 30 minutes each day on ___ process? An hour? More than an hour?"

◆ "Based on what we've discussed so far, how do you think this new process will affect your job?"

◆ "What do you think you need to be successful with this new process change?"

◆ "How do you think that you can begin to implement this process change now?"

Asking an open-ended question is an excellent way of getting the participants involved in the meeting, increases the energy level of the session, and generates group synergy. Open-ended questions often start with

◆ "Tell me about . . . "
◆ "Why . . . "
◆ "What do you think about . . . "
◆ "How . . . "

Usually questions that start this way help the participants to expound on their answers, revealing information that can be helpful in discussion.

Close-Ended Questions

Close-ended questions are sometimes preferable to open-ended ones in certain situations. Closed-ended questions are excellent for getting at specific facts and information.

For example, what if group participants are expected to read information about the new process change prior to attending the presentation. You could ask a closed-ended question requiring a yes or no response to gauge how many read the information such as: "How many of you had a chance to read the information that I sent last week about the new process change?" You aren't interested at this point in whether they agree with or are excited about the change or not, only the percentage of the group that has some baseline understanding of the topic to be discussed. Closed questions often begin with

◆ "Who . . . ?"
◆ "Where . . . "
◆ "When . . . "
◆ "Did you . . . "

Hypothetical Questions

Hypothetical questions are great to get people thinking freely in situations in which many answers may be valid. They often start with "What if . . . ?"

For example, "What if we could implement a new process regarding _____ that would reduce the amount of time you spend on that task by 50 percent every day?" or "Where do you think this process will affect your workflow the most each day?"

Hypothetical questions are excellent discussion starters because they allow the participants to internalize a situation; think through any issues, problems, or solutions; and then actively discuss the impact and their ideas. One warning—because hypothetical discussions are so effective at getting the audience to open up and join in the discussion, as a facilitator you may need to rein things in a bit to meet the agenda time constraints.

Rhetorical Questions

Rhetorical questions—while really not questions at all—are used primarily to get the group thinking when you don't really expect them to answer the question aloud. These types of questions are used primarily for effect and to create excitement or interest in the topics and discussions to come.

For example, "We've all heard about the new process change, and I know that change is sometimes difficult. But have I told you that this new process has been proven to reduce workflow downtime by 50 percent?"

The success of rhetorical questions, just like the other facilitation techniques discussed in this section, is directly related to how you ask the question as much as what you ask. When using this technique, vary the pace of your speech to emphasize key words and then end with silence. Allow the participants time to process what you have said because rhetorical questions are a great way to prime a group to discuss a topic.

Guided Discussion

Guided discussions are a type of structured exercise that enable facilitators to ask the group a series of planned questions designed to get them to wrestle with topics and issues at a deeper level. As they answer the questions, the facilitator summarizes their content and may also play devil's advocate to drive for deeper content or application, and guides the discussion to the next question.

POINTER

Carefully select the participants to invite to the facilitation session. People's time is a valuable resource. Select the participants most likely to contribute and who can help achieve the desired business outcomes. When creating the list, consider who is required to attend and who is optional.

Storytelling

Storytelling is an interesting, proven, and inexpensive way to prepare examples from your own experiences. Stories are often memorable, people like to hear them, and they tend to be a useful technique to capture an audience's attention and illustrate key points.

We all know presenters, facilitators, and leaders who seem to have an innate ability to tell stories. They are able to pull out an appropriate tale, with a poignant message, just right for the situation or audience at hand. The art of good storytelling is a learned skill that comes with practice. You can start a story to get discussions going and leave the rest of the story for later. Or, you can begin the story and then ask the group, "What do you think happened next?"

When thinking through story development, remember a good story has a beginning and an end. Consider the best point in time to begin your story, and develop an engaging start to draw in participants. Think about the pinnacle moments in the story, and how you can leverage them for maximum impact. And of course, your story should have a natural and clear ending. Practice telling the story a few times prior to the facilitation session.

Perhaps the most important characteristic of an effective storyteller is the ability to remain authentic—that is, staying true to your own stories and maintaining the integrity of stories you select to retell. This means sharing truthful and relevant facts and detail.

Authenticity also shows up on your face. When you are truly engaged in the story, the group can tell by your facial expressions and body language. By sharing the emotion you feel in the telling of the story, you help the audience resonate with you and your key point.

Winging it with examples and stories doesn't work. You can get off schedule in a big way. If you select a story to tell on the spot, you might be stealing your thunder for an important point later. You might get to the end only to discover that the main point isn't really relevant to the content at hand. Some presenters even get to the end of a spur-of-the-moment story and realize that not only does it not make a point, but also that the punch line is offensive. Think through your telling of examples and stories before you begin.

Humor

Humor and laughter help improve, maintain, and enhance participant interest in a facilitation session. Camaraderie begins to develop when the facilitator and participants share a pun, story, or other common experience. Humor fosters a "team" atmosphere and promotes a positive experience.

Here are some tips for using humor, jokes, and funny stories during facilitation sessions:

- ◆ The humorous item must be relevant to the session topics and discussion at hand. Telling a story or joke just for fun takes the facilitation session off track.
- ◆ Avoid humor that might offend or alienate participants. Make sure your joke or story is clean. Perhaps this cautionary note seems obvious, but for some facilitators, it isn't. Using even mild curse words is offensive to some members of the audience and makes you look unprofessional. Don't think that if your audience swears, you can too. Part of your role as a facilitator is to model professional behavior.
- ◆ Laugh at yourself, particularly when a story or pun flops. This puts the participants at ease and indicates that you are comfortable with the group and self-confident about your facilitation skills.

Quotations

Quotations from others that are strategically planned in the beginning, middle, or end of your facilitation session often have the effect of stimulating people's thinking. Before you use a quote, however, be sure of its authenticity—especially if you found it on-line—and its relevance to the subject matter. When you use a quote, always give attribution to the appropriate source.

Metaphors

Metaphors, as well as analogies and anecdotes, are thought-provoking forms of speech that open people's minds to think differently about a subject or issue. According to *Webster's Eleventh New Collegiate Dictionary*, a metaphor is a "figure of speech in which a word or phrase literally denoting one kind of object or idea is used in place of another to suggest a likeness or analogy between them" (Merriam-Webster, 2005).

One presenter at a career development seminar used the New York marathon as a metaphor for the effort involved in searching for a new job. As he planted a picture in the minds of his audience of the daunting task of running the marathon, he explained that conducting a job search was similar because those who are success-ful in completing the journey in the shortest time are always the ones who spent the most time preparing themselves.

Analogies

An analogy, according to Webster's, is a "resemblance in some par-ticulars between things otherwise unlike" (Merriam-Webster, 2005). Analogies, like metaphors, often help paint a picture in people's minds that help people to "see" concepts or ideas more clearly. One facilitator, wanting to lay the foundation for introducing the agenda with regard to a new financial reporting system, used this analogy: "My understanding is that trying to reconcile the old monthly financial reports was like putting together a jigsaw puzzle only to find some of the pieces missing." Nodding their heads in agreement, the participants became eager, wanting to learn more about this new, less frustrating system and the project.

Using Tables and Graphs

To help participants in a facilitation session understand data or statistical information, consider using a table to organize the information. Be prepared to clarify (or have an expert available who can clarify) the statistical meaning of the data and the implications, and provide sources if necessary. Be sure to proofread the table data and ensure the accuracy of the numbers and calculations.

Graphs are an effective way to present data, show trends, and demonstrate relationships. However, some graphs are more effective at accomplishing these goals than others. In general:

- **Bar graphs**—show relationships between two or more variables at one time or at several points in time. Improve the readability of a bar chart by making the bars wider than the spaces between them. Don't make graphs too complicated—readability and the ability to understand the information are the keys to making the graph of value to the participants. As a general guideline, the audience should be able to read and understand the graph in fewer than 30 seconds.

- **Line graphs**—show a progression of changes over time. Be sure to label axes, data lines, and data points clearly. Be careful not to exaggerate the data points by changing the scale (for example, 0–100 or 1–50) or gridlines in the background to make something look more significant than it really is. Tick marks often clutter a graph—so use them sparingly and only if they add clarity for the audience. Gridlines or other graph elements that do not add clarity should be omitted.

- **Pie charts**—show the relationships between the parts of a unit at a given moment. Include only essential information in pie charts and avoid having more than six wedges of the pie. Smaller pie slices can always be lumped into an "other" category.

Debriefing Sessions

The facilitator leads a large-group guided discussion after a structured exercise or activity is complete. The debriefing discussion is designed to gather insights from the activity, summarize the main points, and help the group to come to agreement.

Planning Effective Closing Activities

The end of a facilitation session is usually what participants remember most, so it is important to make the ending a memorable one. Take the time to plan the closing activity. The length of time required for this segment of the facilitation session depends on the length of the session itself. For example, a four-hour facilitation session may have a 15-minute closing activity, whereas a two-day session may require an hour for the close. A good closing activity should accomplish these goals:

- **Review and summarize**—take a few minutes to summarize and review what was covered during the session. Go over the agenda points and indicate what you covered, what was not covered, and any possible items for another meeting.

- **Discuss outstanding questions**—allow at least five minutes of question time at the end of the session summary to ensure that everyone has the same perception of the meeting as you do and there are no points of confusion.

- **Gain agreements and commitments from participants**— end the session with the group agreeing on the contents and outcomes of the meeting. In addition, each person should have made a commitment to further action. Make sure that each person is able to state what he or she is going to do and when. Plan to follow up at a later date.

◆ **Evaluate the session**—periodically distribute an evaluation form to maintain and improve the facilitation session quality.

◆ **End on time** (or better yet—a few minutes early!)—show that you respect the participants' time and end the meeting when the agenda said it would end. If there are agenda points that did not get covered, then plan to have another meeting. If possible, end on a high note and always thank the group for their time and participation!

Now that you have an appreciation for the various facilitation techniques to use in your session, Worksheet 3.1 will help you determine those facilitation skills that come easily to you and those that need attention.

WORKSHEET 3.1
Facilitation Techniques Self-Assessment

Use this self-assessment to plan additional skill development by critiquing your confidence level in each of the facilitation methods listed below. For areas of low confidence, identify specific actions you plan to take to improve in that area.

FACILITATION TECHNIQUE	CONFIDENCE LEVEL			ACTIONS
	Low	Moderate	High	
1. Assessing participants' current knowledge	❏	❏	❏	
2. Engaging participants in discussions and activities	❏	❏	❏	
3. Sequencing discussions and activities	❏	❏	❏	
4. Providing activity instructions	❏	❏	❏	
5. Allotting and adjusting time	❏	❏	❏	
6. Choosing and managing group and subgroup sizes	❏	❏	❏	
7. Providing feedback	❏	❏	❏	
8. Using transitions	❏	❏	❏	
9. Adjusting on the fly	❏	❏	❏	
10. Using questioning techniques	❏	❏	❏	
11. Controlling discussions	❏	❏	❏	
12. Remaining neutral in debates	❏	❏	❏	

Worksheet 3.1, continued

FACILITATION TECHNIQUE	CONFIDENCE LEVEL			ACTIONS
	Low	Moderate	High	
13. Avoiding winging it	❐	❐	❐	
14. Affirming	❐	❐	❐	
15. Watching and responding to body language	❐	❐	❐	
16. Being comfortable with, and capitalizing on, silence	❐	❐	❐	
17. Gaining consensus and agreement	❐	❐	❐	
18. Conducting debriefing sessions	❐	❐	❐	

STEP 3

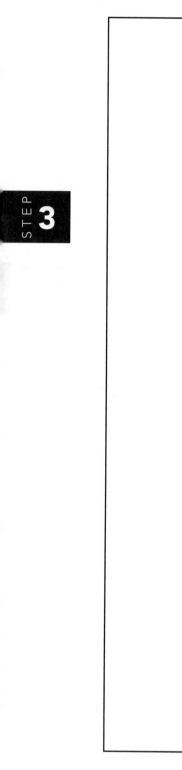

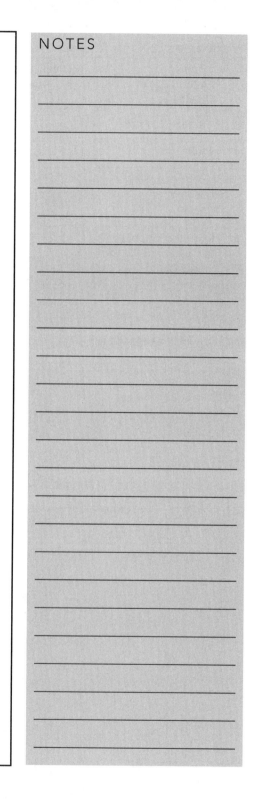

NOTES

Use Tools and Techniques to Engage Participants

OVERVIEW

Systematic decision making

Problem-solving model

Types of facilitation tools

Group appropriateness

Effective team decision making doesn't just happen—it's hard work! A large percentage of a facilitator's time is spent helping teams make decisions. This entails generating the ideas for solutions and then selecting the best answer offered by the team. This chapter describes a number of methods and techniques to facilitate group problem solving and decision making.

Systematic Decision Making

The fact is, groups are notoriously inefficient and often ineffective at solving problems and making decisions. The reasons for this include the following:

◆ Organizations address simple, routine tasks with few key stakeholders by using procedures or standards, which often allows individual autonomy. The problems appropriate for team consideration, however, are a different breed. Organizations convene work groups to complete inherently

Factors Influencing Group Participation

A number of factors influence how much and at what level people participate in team meetings

- level of self-confidence
- knowledge of the topic
- degree of familiarity with others in the group
- level in the organization
- fear of looking like a fool
- opportunity to grandstand.

For groups with particularly dominant or quiet individuals, consider techniques that promote relatively equal participation among all group members.

complex, novel, or territorially volatile tasks—with no problem-solving method to follow.

- For the "two heads are better than one" approach to succeed, team members must have adequate methods, techniques, and tools at their disposal. If they do not have these, a group will not complete a complex task as well as its best member could have—had he or she been left alone to solve the problem. Yet, teams are frequently unaware of, or unpracticed in, the use of problem-solving methods, techniques, and tools. Organizations often assemble groups with unrealistic expectations that group members are smart enough to figure the problem out on their own.

- Because groups are unpracticed in the use of problem-solving methods, there is ample opportunity in group meetings to get side-tracked, to form competing alliances, and to permit emotionalism to run amok.

One of the main reasons teams encounter difficulty in dealing with problems is that they fail to follow an organized procedure. Teams should have an agreed-upon process for making decisions.

Problem-Solving Model

Consider using this model to provide a formal problem-solving and decision-making process when facilitating groups.

Step 1: Identify and Define the Problem

One of the advantages of a group is that its members have widely different perspectives and their understanding of the problem being considered can vary significantly. If not adequately managed, however, this advantage can become a disadvantage. At this stage, the group should focus on:

- Being explicit about the language used and what it means. Participants should provide specific descriptions and examples.
- Determining no more than six or seven goals.
- Questioning assumptions and perceptions.

An often-overlooked step in the process—developing clear definitions—is critical because the effectiveness of the rest of the process requires all participants to have a clear, common understanding and language when discussing issues and problems.

For example, you are facilitating a group of environmentalists and commercial developers addressing land-use policy in a wilderness area. Each subgroup emotionally argues its position for and against a change in policy until you press the subgroups for a definition of "wilderness." Each has a different operational interpretation of the term. When they come to a common understanding of the term, many of the apparently unmanageable differences evaporate.

POINTER

Facilitators need to follow formal problem-solving and decision-making processes to help groups achieve defined goals and objectives. Following a structured process ensures that crucial steps are not skipped or overlooked.

STEP **4**

Be explicit about the language used and what it means. Make participants provide specific descriptions and examples to ensure that everyone is using apples-to-apples definitions, and all are on the same page.

Step 2: Research and Analyze the Problem

Sometimes the problems a group must address are not obvious to all participants, and the solutions may be viewed in different ways. Groups rarely make decisions in an empirical vacuum. Intelligence involves gathering relevant data, both objective and subjective, that is pertinent to the decision the group must make. As new data emerge, it is common to see the problem redefined.

Step 3: Establish Criteria and Evaluate Solutions

You make nonprogrammed, rational decisions by evaluating options using one or more criteria. Frequently, however, criteria are not made explicit, so the reasons an individual has for preferring one option to another remain hidden to the group members. The resulting consequence is that the group perceives this person's preference as somewhat irrational.

For a group to succeed in making decisions, group members must make public and explicit the criteria that are important to them. And because all criteria are not equal, you also need to determine the relative importance or weight of each criterion.

Step 4: Explore and Generate Alternatives

Teams often begin the process with this step; however, an effective team will resist that temptation and move systematically through the process and accomplish the first three steps before tackling Step 4.

If the group has done that, members already understand the problems or issues, have researched information and gathered the facts, and have established evaluation criteria and relative importance. Now it's time to get all thinking caps on and generate a variety of ideas and solutions.

When promoting idea generation, successful facilitators encourage groups to consider all possible options. This means stating the ground rules of not criticizing or discounting any ideas at this point in the process and not to settle too quickly on any one option.

As a facilitator, be careful that participants are not settling too soon—that is, choosing a solution that seems to solve the problem without continuing to look for a better solution. Although one solution may be adequate, superior solutions stem from thinking that is initially divergent—creatively exploring possible solutions before agreeing on any one choice. There are two types of solutions:

- solutions that are mutually exclusive
- solutions that can be combined.

Too often, groups treat solutions as "either/or," rather than "both/and," which results in unnecessary polarization when you might be able to compromise.

Step 5: Evaluate and Choose the Best Solution

This stage involves systematically evaluating each potentially viable option against the criteria and choosing the "best" options (that is, the ones that stack up best against the criteria).

Successful facilitators verify that everyone is clear about what is meant by each idea or solution. Without a clear understanding of the proposed solutions, the group will falter when trying to evaluate and narrow down the options in search of the best solution.

This is the appropriate point in the process for the group to now become critical about the ideas generated.

At this final step in the process, successful facilitators help the group clarify discussions, summarize the results of evaluating and narrowing solutions, keep the group on track, and reach consensus so that everyone "buys in" to the final decision.

Types of Facilitation Tools

Effective team decision making depends on defining the problem. Simply stated, a problem is a discrepancy between what is and what should be. A problem should be stated in the form of a question. "How can we reduce the number of defective widgets produced daily?" is a better way to consider the problem than "Develop a plan to reduce scrap material."

Depending on where the group is in the problem-solving and decision-making process, facilitators use different tools to support and guide the group as well as the process. Table 4.1 lists categories of tools to facilitate idea generation, problem definition, problem analysis, and decision making.

When selecting the appropriate tool, facilitators need to consider:

- What step in the process is the group in?
- Are they trying to generate ideas, evaluate ideas, or come to an agreement on the best solution?

STEP 4

TABLE 4.1
Facilitator Tools by Process Step

Purpose	Tools	Page
Identifying and Generating Ideas	◆ Brainstorming	60
	◆ Sticky Note Brainstorming	61
	◆ Round Robins	62
	◆ Card Tricks	62
	◆ Brainwriting	63
	◆ Mind Mapping	64
	◆ Fish Bone Diagramming	64
Defining and Analyzing Problems	◆ Mind Mapping	64
	◆ Fish Bone Diagramming	64
	◆ SWOT Analysis	66
	◆ 5-Why Technique	68
Listing and Prioritizing Solutions	◆ Affinity Diagrams	69
	◆ Nominal Group Technique	71
	◆ Multivoting Technique	71
	◆ Dots	72
	◆ Spectrum Listening	73
	◆ Consensus Cards	73
	◆ Matrixes and Decision Tables	74
Decision Making	◆ Force Field Analyses	74
	◆ Pros and Cons Lists	76
	◆ Voting	77

STEP 4

The group dynamics may also affect the best tool to guide the group. This next section details each tool and technique and the guidelines for implementing them.

Brainstorming

In brainstorming, the idea is to come up with as many ideas as possible and then whittle them down to a couple that seem the most promising. Brainstorming promotes collaborative problem solving by getting the audience or small groups to focus on creating and expanding a list of possibilities.

The number of people who can participate has no limit, but presenters often break larger audiences into subgroups of four to five participants to create and expand a list of possible ideas or solutions. In brainstorming, record and recognize all ideas, no matter how outlandish. Postpone evaluation of ideas put forward until the next step in the process.

How to Use

Brainstorming is an excellent way to engage participants by posing a problem for which you want them to develop solutions or to generate a list of ideas related to a specific topic. When facilitating brainstorming, use these steps:

1. Assign a question or get the groups to agree on a central question related to the topic.
2. Each participant in the group needs to suggest at least one idea or solution to the question posed.
3. Have one person in each group capture all ideas generated—no matter how outlandish. Postpone evaluation of ideas put forward until the next step in the process.

POINTER

STEP 4

Brainstorming Ground Rules

Remind participants of the brainstorming ground rules prior to beginning a brainstorming session:

- ◆ No criticism of an idea is allowed.
- ◆ Strive for the longest list possible—go for quantity.
- ◆ Strive for creativity—"wild and crazy" ideas are encouraged!
- ◆ Build on the ideas of others—"hitchhike" or "piggyback."

---

4. Call time.

5. Depending on the purpose of the brainstorming session, have the groups either go back and select the top five ideas to develop further and refine—or—go back and generate ideas for each solution posed.

6. Have the groups review the completed list for clarity and duplication, and then make their final recommendations.

Sticky Note Brainstorming

One variation on traditional brainstorming includes using sticky notes to capture individually brainstormed ideas. The notes are then placed on a wall for everyone to see. This enables the participants to easily group the ideas by topic, category, feasibility, and so on.

How to Use

This activity is especially useful for getting participants on their feet and moving around and makes it easy to group, prioritize, or whittle down ideas. Use these steps to implement this technique:

1. Provide participants with several large sticky notes (or index cards) and markers.

2. Direct the group to brainstorm and to legibly jot down one idea on each sticky note. If you try to gather contrasting information (for example, problems and solutions), perhaps have the participants document the information on different-colored notes or cards).

3. Instruct the group to place their sticky note ideas on the wall (or within categories on a flipchart, and so on).
   - ◆ **Tip:** If you are trying to maintain anonymity, then collect the ideas and post them on the wall or flipchart yourself.

4. Ask the participants to come up and read all of the ideas.

5. Begin the group discussion and evaluation process to organize the ideas and begin whittling down the list.

Round Robins

In this technique, the facilitator gives each person an opportunity to state orally one idea pertinent to the question posed. Round robins encourage relatively equal participation among all group members.

How to Use

1. Pose a question to the group.
2. Give the group time to ponder the question and generate at least one idea. Stress that they may want to come up with several ideas in case there are duplicates. The goal is to generate new ideas.
3. Call time.
4. Either ask for a volunteer or call on one person to state his or her idea, which is recorded publicly on a whiteboard or flipchart.
5. Go to the next group member and continue the process of asking for ideas and posting them. If any members have more than one idea, they need to wait until their next turn to express each idea.
6. Continue the round robin until all ideas have been stated.

Card Tricks

In some situations, people may be reluctant to express their ideas orally. For example, in a meeting with participants from all hierarchy levels in the organization, certain group participants may be intimidated, fearful that those higher in the chain of command will

POINTER

Use various questioning techniques. Questioning techniques are a staple of any successful facilitator. Each type of question (open-ended, close-ended, Socratic, rhetorical, hypothetical, and so on) serves a different purpose to engage participants and encourage discussion.

judge their ideas negatively. Or, if the topic is particularly sensitive, participants may be reluctant to express their views or ideas publicly.

How to Use

1. Pose a question to the group.
2. Give the group time to ponder the question and generate at least one idea. Direct participants to anonymously jot down their ideas on paper, index cards, sticky notes, and so on.
3. Call time.
4. Collect the cards and read them to the group. The goal is for the cloak of anonymity to generate more and creative ideas than if participants were to state the ideas publicly.

STEP **4**

Brainwriting

This technique generates a large number of ideas or solutions. The underlying principle is that the greater number of ideas generated, the greater the possibility that a quality solution will be identified. This "piggybacking" or "hitchhiking" approach enables participants to benefit from the ideas of others and to generate new ideas.

How to Use

1. Break the group into teams of four to six members.
2. Pose a question, problem, or issue. Direct participants to individually come up with as many responses as possible and to write them on paper. No discussion is allowed.
3. Call time.
4. Ask the participants to pass their responses to someone else in the group (for example, everyone pass to the right, left, and so on) or to place their papers in the middle of the table and exchange them for someone else's.
5. Instruct the individuals to use the lists as inspiration and to try to generate additional ideas or modifications.
6. Continue to exchange, still in silence, until the agreed-upon time limit is reached.

7. Collect the papers. Review and evaluate the ideas at a later time.

Mind Mapping

This technique is also called idea mapping, clustering, webbing, and spidering. It is a fast, fun method of free association that produces ideas. It helps members suspend judgment of ideas and can be used either individually or in a group. An example of mind mapping is given in Figure 4.1.

How to Use

1. Instruct participants to write a word or phrase on a piece of paper that describes the problem.
2. Draw a circle around the problem statement.
3. For two minutes, write down all aspects of the problem.
4. Connect the related words with arrows or lines.
5. Look for three or four main themes or categories, and assign a geometric symbol (for example, a square, circle, triangle, diamond) to each category.
6. Discuss the findings.

Fish Bone Diagramming

Sometimes stating the problem and clarifying it in a brief discussion is sufficient. Often, however, this is not enough, and you need more formal techniques to help the group work toward an understanding of the problem. One helpful technique is called a fish bone diagram—also known as an Ishakawa diagram or cause-and-effect diagram.

Fish bone diagrams emerged from the practice of quality assurance as a way of graphically identifying the factors affecting quality. In this context, facilitators use it as a way of identifying specifics that influence the desired outcome. For example, a group of executives looking at declining sales might incorrectly (or prematurely) conclude that the decline results from inadequate marketing of the new products and services available. Rather than

FIGURE 4.1
Mind Mapping

▶ Group Process Tools

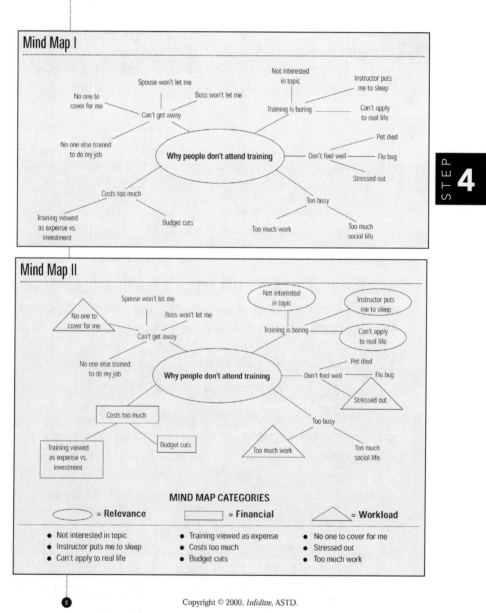

Mind Map I

Why people don't attend training

Spouse won't let me
Boss won't let me
No one to cover for me
Can't get away
No one else trained to do my job
Not interested in topic
Instructor puts me to sleep
Training is boring
Can't apply to real life
Pet died
Don't feel well — Flu bug
Stressed out
Costs too much
Too busy
Training viewed as expense vs. investment
Budget cuts
Too much work
Too much social life

Mind Map II

Why people don't attend training

Spouse won't let me
Boss won't let me
No one to cover for me
Can't get away
No one else trained to do my job
Not interested in topic
Instructor puts me to sleep
Training is boring
Can't apply to real life
Pet died
Don't feel well — Flu bug
Stressed out
Costs too much
Too busy
Training viewed as expense vs. investment
Budget cuts
Too much work
Too much social life

MIND MAP CATEGORIES

⬭ = Relevance   ▭ = Financial   △ = Workload

- Not interested in topic
- Instructor puts me to sleep
- Can't apply to real life

- Training viewed as expense
- Costs too much
- Budget cuts

- No one to cover for me
- Stressed out
- Too much work

jumping to conclusions, the group could use a fish bone diagram to examine the range of factors that might be causing the problem. Figure 4.2 offers an example of a fish bone diagram.

How to Use

1. The group lists any and all factors related to the question or problem posed.
2. The group places the factors into categories, such as marketing, sales compensation, motivation, product design, customer satisfaction, and so on.
3. The group begins to fill in the diagram.
4. Each major branch (for example, marketing, customer satisfaction, and so forth) represents one of the categories. The steps connected to the branch represent the more particular items from the original list. As the diagram grows, additional ideas emerge and the group adds them to the diagram.

What frequently happens is that one of two branches receives more attention than the others, and the group has an "a-ha" experience. Participants see the problem in a different light.

SWOT Analysis

A SWOT (**s**trengths, **w**eaknesses, **o**pportunities, **t**hreats) analysis—also known as an internal and external environmental analysis—is used to determine strengths and weaknesses (internal) and opportunities and threats (external) of a particular situation. Another purpose of this analysis is to identify the contingencies that aid and prevent an organization, department, group, or individuals from achieving a particular set of goals.

For example, a SWOT analysis considers

◆ **internal environmental factors**—including an organization's financial condition, managerial abilities and attitudes, facilities, staffing size and quality, competitive position, image, and structure

FIGURE 4.2

Fish Bone Diagram

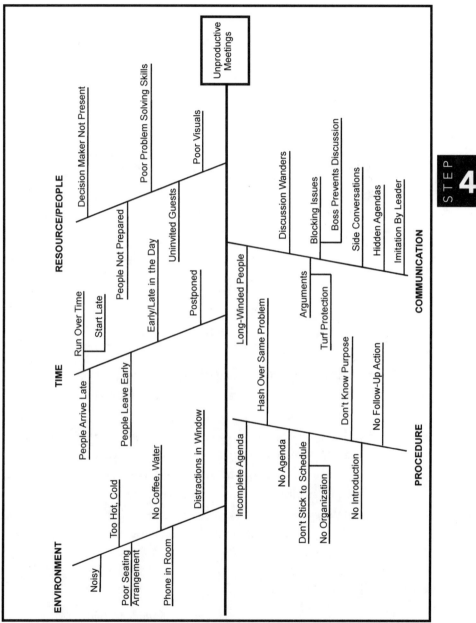

◆ **external environmental factors**—including an organization's economic condition, legal and political realities, social and cultural values, the state of technology, the
availability of resources, and the organization's competitive structure.

This technique is helpful in creating background analysis for solving a problem.

How to Use

1. Create and display the chart below.

Strengths	Weaknesses

Opportunities	Threats

2. Use brainstorming or any idea-generation technique to
   have the group generate a list of ideas for each quadrant
   on the chart.
3. Using probing questions to get the group to delve into the
   details, define and explicitly explain their thoughts and rationale, and discuss the ideas at a deeper level.
4. Confirm with the group if they are ready to make a
   decision.
5. Use any of the techniques to gain consensus from the
   group.

5-Why Technique

The 5-why technique is a popular tool that tends to tell the story
of causes and effects, starting from back to front. It provides detail

and is useful with complex problems that stem from multiple or contributing causes.

How to Use

1. Write down the problem.
2. Ask the group to answer the question, "Why does this happen?"
3. Document the answers.
4. Turn each answer into the next why question (for example, "Why does this happen?").
5. Repeat for five iterations.

Keep track of relationships between cause statements and the next level of why.

Affinity Diagrams

Affinity diagrams (also referred to as affinity maps or groups) gather a large number of ideas, organize these ideas into logical groupings based on the natural relationships between items, and define groups of items. A follow-up to the affinity diagram is the interrelationship diagram, which charts cause-and-effect relationships among the groupings. They are best used when issues seem too complex and relationships among facts seem confusing, when thoughts or facts are ambiguous or in chaos, or when the group needs to discover the major themes contained in a great number of ideas.

How to Use

1. Phrase the issue to be considered. The issue should be broad, neutral, clearly stated, and well understood by the group convened to discuss it.
2. Generate or record ideas. Working silently, each individual records his or her ideas in response to the issue or question on sticky notes (one idea per note). The group members hold all ideas until the next step.

3. Place notes on a specified surface. Without discussing their ideas, team members move to a specially prepared wall (covered with flipchart or butcher paper) or another flat surface and place the completed notes on the prepared surface. At this point, the notes are placed randomly on the surface.

4. Sort ideas into related groups. When all of the notes are placed on the surface, the group members, working in silence and moving quickly, use their "gut reactions" to move notes into related groups. Individuals can move any note anywhere on the surface. Disputes or disagreements about placement of notes are resolved silently. After an interval, the group is allowed to discuss their notes and finalize the groupings.

5. Create the category title. When all ideas are located in a category of related ideas, the group identifies the one idea or note that captures the essence of all the ideas in that group. This category title is written on the surface and lines are drawn to enclose all ideas related to that title.

6. Next, the group looks for interrelationships among the categories. The group examines the categories to explore relationships. This step in the process involves looking at each category and comparing it to other categories and then asking the questions, "What is the relationship between these two? Which category causes or influences the rest?" If a relationship exists between two categories, the group draws a line that links the categories and notes the direction of the cause-and-effect relationship with an arrow.

7. Identify the key drivers. The last step in the interrelationship diagram involves identifying the categories that are the primary drivers or influencers. For each category, total up the number of outgoing and incoming arrows and write the totals next to each category. The categories with the greatest influence—the primary drivers or causes—are those with the most outgoing arrows. Those with the most incoming arrows tend to be the results or effects of other forces on the page and therefore not a high-leverage

choice for effecting change in the outcomes. The purpose of this activity is to focus on the factors that have the greatest influence on the issue.

The outcomes of affinity and interrelationship diagrams are large groups of ideas that are categorized into related clusters of ideas, each with a clear title, and with the relationships clearly drawn. Furthermore, the key drivers or influencers are identified as a first step in developing a high-leverage strategy for causing lasting change in the system.

Multivoting, or Nominal Group Technique

Multivoting or nominal group technique is a structured method that a team can use to brainstorm a wide range of responses to an issue, clarify each of the responses, and rank the responses from most to least important. Facilitators often use this technique with a team of representative stakeholders to minimize the impact of team dynamics in generating, evaluating, and ranking or selecting interventions.

How to Use

1. Agree on and write on a flipchart the issue facing the team. Post it so all can see it. Ensure that everyone understands the issue.
2. Ask each team member to develop a written list of ideas or suggestions. This is done individually, privately, and silently. Note that team members should record all their ideas, rejecting none.
3. After list making is completed, ask each participant—in a round-robin fashion—to offer one idea from his or her list. As each person responds, record the idea on a flipchart and number each item. Individuals may skip ideas already offered by someone else. Continue in rounds until the team has offered all its ideas.
4. After all ideas are recorded, lead the group in clarifying, linking, discussing, or eliminating ideas. Make notations

on the flipchart to help improve understanding of each issue. The group should be aware that it is not necessary to agree that an issue is important; agreement is only needed on the meaning of the issue. The goal of this step is to reduce the list to a single roster of distinct, well-defined ideas.

5. Participants review the list and select their top five priority items. Each member notes on paper ballots the number of the item and a word or phrase that describes the item (one item per ballot). Then each team member rank orders the ballots from five (most important) to one (least important).

6. The team gives its ballots to the facilitator who records the numbers (five through one) from the ballots on the flipchart pages next to the item receiving a vote.

7. Total the points for each item. The item that receives the most points is ranked most important by the entire group.

The outcome of multivoting or nominal group technique is a rank-ordered list of causes or solutions—each clearly defined and understood by group members.

Dots

This is a simple and time-efficient method for voting on ideas or solutions. It ensures that all members are actively involved, and it presents a visual representation of areas of consensus.

How to Use

1. List all of the previously generated ideas on a flipchart or large sheets of paper.
2. Give each participant an allotment of self-adhesive, colored dots.
3. Instruct participants to vote for ideas by placing a colored dot next to each idea. Dots can be allocated in any manner. For example, if each person is given 10 dots, all of the dots may be placed next to one idea, or three dots

may be placed next to one idea and seven dots placed next to another.

4. Tally the votes. The ideas receiving the greatest number of votes are selected for further analysis or implementation.

Spectrum Listening

This technique provides a mechanism for analyzing the major advantages and blocks to the group's ideas and suggestions. Rather than viewing the ideas as good or bad, spectrum listening encourages participants to hear and evaluate each idea thoroughly by listening for, and making statements about, three key areas.

How to Use

1. Have a participant present an idea.
2. Ask the group to listen for and make statements about:
   ◆ What I like about the idea
   ◆ What concerns I have about the idea
   ◆ How my concerns can be turned into opportunities.
3. Discuss and evaluate the idea.

Consensus Cards

For this technique, group members use red, yellow, or green cards to show their position on an issue at any point during the discussion. The consensus card is made of construction paper folded and glued or taped into a hollow triangle. The "face" of each side of the hollow triangle is red ("I disagree"), yellow ("I can live with the decision"), or green ("I agree"). When all participants have shown the card with the same color, either red, yellow, or green, they have reached a consensus.

How to Use

1. Define the issue or problem.
2. Instruct the participants to place the yellow face toward the center of the table.

3. Discuss the solutions. When asked, the participants may change their card faces to indicate their positions on the topic.

4. Discussion stops when all are in agreement (that is, all cards have the same color cards showing).

Matrixes or Weighted Decision Tables

This method helps evaluate solutions against predetermined criteria. A major advantage of this method is that it recognizes the relative importance of each criterion.

How to Use

1. List the alternatives.
2. Brainstorm the decision criteria.
3. Evaluate the decision criteria and determine the importance of each item.
4. Construct a matrix table (see Table 4.2 for an example).
5. List the criteria across the top and the potential solutions down the left-hand side of the matrix.
6. Using a scale of one to seven, with one being low importance and seven being high importance, ask the group to assign a value to each criterion.
7. Using the same rating scale, ask the team to rate each idea against each criterion. Record the rating in the upper portion of the diagonal line.
8. Multiply the rating for each idea by the weight given to each criterion, and write the product in the lower portion of the diagonal line.
9. Add the products for each idea and write the sum in the total score column.
10. The idea with the highest total score is the group's choice.

Force Field Analyses

Kurt Lewin (1890–1947)—sometimes called the grandfather of organization development because of his profound effect on the field—

TABLE 4.2
Sample Matrix: Site Selection

CRITERION	Availability of Parking	Proximity to Public Transportation	Rental Fee	Capacity to Accommodate a Large Group	TOTAL
Criterion Rating	5	5	7	3	
Site A	4 / 20	1 / 5	3 / 21	7 / 21	67
Site B	5 / 25	6 / 30	3 / 21	5 / 15	91
Site C	3 / 15	5 / 25	2 / 14	6 / 18	70

From Barbara Darraugh, "Group Process Tools," *Infoline* No. 259407, pp. 9–10 (ASTD Press, 1997).

defined two factors: driving and restraining forces. These forces either work for or against a particular change. The goal is to maximize positive change forces, known as "driving forces," and to minimize or eliminate the negative ones, known as "resisting forces." Facilitators use force field analysis to encourage driving forces and discourage restraining forces.

How to Use

1. Create and display the group's goal statement of what needs to be achieved in the chart below.

Goal Statement:

Driving Forces Factors that Work Toward Our Goal	Restraining Forces Factors that Work Against Our Goal

2. Use brainstorming to generate ideas and to gain agreement on the specific driving and restraining factors that move the group toward the desired goal.
3. After compiling a list of ideas for both sides of the chart, work with the group to agree on the two or three driving forces to maximize as well as two or three restraining forces to minimize.
4. Brainstorm and list the steps for the actions required to strengthen or decrease the forces identified.

Pros and Cons Lists

Facilitators often use lists of pros and cons to help groups evaluate solutions and to determine the best option or combination of options. The technique enables the group to look at all aspects of a solution before deciding whether or not to implement it.

How to Use

1. Create and display the chart below.

Pros	Cons

2. Use brainstorming to have the group generate a list of pros and cons for a particular solution.
3. Instruct the group to evaluate the list and to comment on whether they are in favor of or against the solution. Try to get the group to delve into the details of the items suggested and discuss at a deeper level.
4. Confirm that the group is ready to make a decision.
5. Use the solution that the group agrees to.

Voting

Voting is a commonly used decision-making method. Although it helps the group to arrive at a quick decision, voting results in winners and losers. There are several types of voting in which each person has one vote including:

- **Simple majority**—the decision is made when more than half of the group chooses the same solution.
- **Super majority**—the decision is made when two-thirds of the group agrees to the same solution.

POINTER

Successful facilitators determine when it is appropriate to convene a group and select suitable decision-making strategies based on an assessment of the problem the group faces.

STEP **4**

Group Appropriateness

No matter which facilitation tool and technique is selected, the most successful facilitators focus on improving group decision making by attending to the following technical issues

- applying structure
- making roles explicit
- using ground rules
- exploring the problems systematically
- employing idea-generation techniques
- using models to evaluate options.

Concentrating on structure does not deny the interpersonal dimension of human decision making. It does, however, help to minimize the unhealthy aspects of emotion that can emerge in the process.

Successful facilitators determine when it is appropriate to convene a group and select suitable decision-making strategies based on an assessment of the problem the group faces. Combined with good meeting protocol, such as adhering to an agenda, facilitators elicit both effectiveness and efficiency in the group's interactions.

Now that basic techniques to facilitate a work group session have been selected, the next step requires facilitators to determine which media and technology to use for greatest impact and achievement of goals.

STEP **4**

Integrate Media and Technology for Impact

OVERVIEW

Understanding benefits of visual aids

Determining which visual aids meet your needs

Selecting appropriate media

Mastering different types of visual aids

STEP **5**

Chances are you'll use at least one type of media to help guide and support the facilitation process. In fact, selecting the media to use is one of the most significant decisions that you will make. Keep in mind that the most important rule is to ensure that the media selected support the session goals and facilitation process.

Visual aids help to make bland, passive sessions come to life by getting participants off their seats, up and moving around as they brainstorm ideas on flipcharts or whiteboards. Presentation software may help to illustrate background information such as process flows and organizational levels.

Because most people have an easier time remembering something they have seen, most facilitation sessions benefit from some use of media. All visuals and materials should be carefully prepared ahead of time to reflect the professionalism of the facilitator and the sponsoring organization, and to convey respect for the group. Therefore, it is important to plan and prepare visual aids carefully to support the facilitation process and not distract from it.

Understanding Benefits of Visual Aids

If you're not quite convinced about the power that visual aids can have, consider this fact: In one study, a presentation that delivered information only verbally achieved a 7 percent comprehension rate; the addition of visuals raised comprehension to 87 percent (cited in Eline, 1997, p. 1).

So aside from helping a group to understand issues, visual aids help to promote clarity, capture ideas, organize and summarize rationale, and facilitate decision making. Moreover, they also

POINTER

Check on meeting logistics. Verify that the room location and arrangement are set up as specified. This includes confirming the number and arrangement of chairs, if meeting-room equipment is available and in working order, and if refreshments have been delivered.

- help you to control the flow and structure of the information to maintain and pique the audience's attention as you reveal the key points and follow a logical decision-making process
- enable the participants to see what something looks like, clarify relationships among numerical data, understand the organizational structure of information, and so on
- provide more clarity when they are organized and thoughtfully integrated
- add interest, variety, and excitement to what might otherwise be a boring meeting.

So which visual aid should you use based on the type of session you need to facilitate?

Determining Which Visual Aids Meet Your Needs

There are many types of visual aids to choose from when planning the facilitation session. You can use whiteboards, posters, flipcharts, transparencies and overhead projectors, slides, presentation software, and so on. There are advantages and disadvantages to each type of visual aid, and some of them lend themselves better to some circumstances than others. Which type of visual aid you choose will depend on the facilitation goals, the makeup of the group, and your budget. The following questions will help you to select the appropriate visual aid:

1. What do you know about the audience (their audience profile) and their expectations for the facilitation session? You need to ensure that any preplanned materials and activities are informative and support the process, but do not confuse or overwhelm the participants.
2. Will sound, motion, color or other effects be required to communicate the message effectively? If you only need to highlight specific points, a transparency or text slides might be sufficient.
3. Under what conditions is the facilitation session taking place? What will be the room size, the size of the group, and the availability of equipment and other media?
4. Do you have the resources—time, money, expertise, and support—to develop appropriate visual aids to their best advantage?

After answering these questions, consider the desired level of interactivity, time of day, and session goals when determining the most appropriate media to support the session.

Selecting Appropriate Media

Keep in mind that the size of the room, the setup and how it supports or hinders movement will dictate the appropriate media for a facilitation session. Media must support the desired level of movement—for example, if you plan to use groups and breakout sessions to encourage participants to be active and move around—then media ties the facilitator or participants to only one part of the room and will not be effective in achieving the type of session you envision.

Your choice of media should also depend on the time of day and the types of activities you plan. For example, your media should appear at the high end of interactivity if it is right after lunch, at the end of the day, or if participants have been sitting passively for a while. Use Table 5.1 to determine which type of media are appropriate based on their ability to support higher and lower interactivity.

Mastering Different Types of Visual Aids

Facilitators have a myriad of visual aids available to plan and conduct an effective and engaging meeting. For example, flipcharts, whiteboards, and overhead transparencies enable participants and you to draw and write information on the fly. Presentation software enables you to create formal, structured, professional-looking

TABLE 5.1

Interactivity Levels Associated with Different Media

Media with Higher Interactivity	Media with Lower Interactivity
◆ Handouts with blanks to be filled in ◆ Flipcharts that participants create themselves ◆ Whiteboards that participants write on themselves ◆ Overhead transparencies, whiteboards, flipcharts with blanks that the facilitator fills in as the discussion continues ◆ Wallboards that participants write on ◆ Walls, flipcharts, or whiteboards that participants post sticky notes on ◆ Physical props that participants can examine and handle	◆ Prepared overhead transparencies, whiteboards, flipcharts, and wallboards ◆ Handouts with all text filled in ◆ Videos, DVDs ◆ Microsoft PowerPoint or presentation software slides, digital presentations, photographic slides ◆ Physical props that only the facilitator handles

presentations. High-tech visual aids such as videotape, digital versatile disks (DVDs), photographic slides, and digital slides can demonstrate or convey information. Despite all of these solutions for enhancing the communication and clarification of information, you need to keep in mind that not all of these options are appropriate all of the time. Visual aids should be used to enhance and support the facilitation process—not dominate the meeting and relegate participants to sit passively on the sideline.

Flipcharts

A flipchart is the most basic visual aid usually consisting of an easel and large pads of paper attached to a flipchart stand or a cardboard backing. You can purchase a variety of flipchart paper—including ones with sticky backs that act like large sticky notes that can be displayed around the room. Other varieties of flipchart paper include blank pages, lined pages, or even grids. Flipcharts are a great resource for smaller group meetings and facilitation sessions, especially for capturing key points from brainstorming sessions or illustrating information on the fly.

Using the Touch, Turn, Talk Method

When working with a flipchart, stand to one side. Which side you stand on depends on which hand you write with. For example, if you are right-handed, stand on the left side of the flipchart (as the participants face it). If you are using tabs to help you navigate within the mass of flipchart pages, position the tabs on the left side as well (again, as the participants face the chart). If you are left-handed, then reverse this stance and placement.

If you see group members craning their necks to see the flipchart, that is your cue to move or to position the flipchart so that everyone can see it more readily.

POINTER

Prepare meeting materials and handouts prior to the meeting. Ensure that they are free of errors (spelling or otherwise) and that you have enough copies for all participants.

STEP 5

POINTER

Flipcharts—one of a facilitator's best tools—should be leveraged extensively to post the agenda, capture parking lot items, diagram problems or issues, post brainstormed ideas, and used to rank or weight solutions to determine a few viable options and much more!

10 Rules When Creating Flipcharts

Consider these points when creating flipcharts:

1. Use a maximum of six lines per page. Use only eight to 10 words per point, and use key words or phrases instead of full sentences. Busy flipcharts obscure your message.

2. Make your letters at least two inches high and verify that the participants can easily read the information from all areas of the room.

3. Use headings on each page to orient the group to the ideas generated, points discussed, and so on. For example, use bold, capital letters for all headings in one color, and show supporting information or ideas as bulleted items in a different color.

4. Especially when creating flipcharts prior to the meeting, use three to four different colors to make them eye-catching and easy to read. Use nontoxic, water-based markers because they smell better, won't bleed through walls and tables, and won't ruin your clothes.

5. If you have to tape flipcharts to a wall for additional writing space, leave one or two blank flipchart pages behind the one you plan to write on to ensure that the marker won't bleed through the paper onto the paint or wallpaper. As a best practice, you can leave a blank sheet of paper between your written flipchart pages so that the participants cannot see what appears on subsequent pages. Use painter's tape to secure paper to the wall so that you don't damage the wall.

6. Use colors that are easy for participants to see—for example, black and blue tend to be the most visible. Use your judgment about using green or red for emphasis. These are great colors to imply "do" and "don't" or "positives" and "negatives," but red can be difficult to see from a distance and some audience members might be colorblind and unable to make the distinction.

7. Lightly, in pencil, at the top corner of each page closest to where you will be standing, write a brief heading of what's on the next page with an arrow under it. This note will help you segue seamlessly to the topics to cover next or material on the following page.

8. Number each page of your flipchart, then mark the corresponding number in your facilitator notes to help you quickly get back on track if you get distracted or lose your place.

9. Always check the spelling of your flipcharts.

10. Use sticky notes, sticky tabs, or clear tape to form tabs at the side of each sheet so that you can quickly navigate to the specific flipchart page you want.

Advantages of Using Flipcharts

As a guideline, use flipcharts in the following situations:

◆ **You want to capture participant ideas and comments—** while professional-looking flipcharts can be created by hand (if you have good hand writing) or printed on large blotters, most facilitators can create effective flipcharts with little effort. For example, use flipcharts during project team meetings to list the top project issues and to facilitate a brainstorming session so you can capture the possible solutions.

◆ **Audience and room size are appropriate**—flipcharts are ideal in rooms with 30 or fewer participants when they are positioned so that everyone has a good line of sight. They provide the participants with the flexibility to display information gathered before the meeting as well as a public

place to capture ideas and questions generated during the
session.

- **Late-afternoon meetings**—flipcharts are especially helpful for meetings conducted immediately after lunch or in
the late afternoon because you do not need to dim the
lights as you would for a slide presentation.

- **You have little or no budget**—flipcharts are a perfect
choice when a last-minute meeting has made its way onto
your calendar and you have little time or budget to prepare a formal presentation with slides or other media. With
flipcharts, you can create the key points, graphs, charts,
or other information to facilitate a meeting almost any
time, anywhere, and on a limited budget.

- **Using flipcharts as a crutch**—because flipcharts can be
created in advance, many facilitators also use them as a
crutch to post an "agenda" of the topics and activities for
quick reference as a reminder of what's next. Other tricks
include writing in pencil on the corners of blank flipchart
pages so that only the facilitator can see the information.
This enables facilitators to appear as though they are posing off-the-cuff questions to the group when in fact the
sequence of the session and the specific questions asked
have been carefully planned in advance of the session.

- **Displaying a visual during the entire meeting**—
flipcharts are particularly effective when you want to display a visual, graph, or chart during the entire session for
you or the participants to refer back to from time to time.

When Not to Use Flipcharts

Flipcharts are not a good idea if your handwriting is barely legible.
To increase your legibility, try printing in block letters using flipchart paper with lines or a grid as a guide. If the audience still
can't read your writing, you may want to try another visual aid.
The bottom line, however, is that if you do not include flipcharts
among your core facilitation tools, then you are depriving yourself—and your participants—of a very useful and unique visual
aid.

Overhead Transparencies

Another useful visual aid is the overhead transparency. Transparencies are similar to flipcharts in that they are low-tech, easy to use, and can be created in a hurry. Colored pens enable you to highlight key points or important words and you can make these decisions on the fly.

Transparencies, however, do require a projector, a projection screen, and electricity, so they are definitely a step up from flipcharts on the technology scale. Because some overhead projectors can project plain paper on the screen—meaning no transparencies are needed—you'll need to verify the type of projector that will be available before you show up for the facilitation session.

POINTER

Plan for media mishaps. For example, if a projector bulb blows, find out where there are spares in advance of the meeting or carry a spare with you.

Using Overhead Transparencies

If the room is small, consider positioning the screen and overhead projector facing one corner rather than straight forward. You'll need to arrange for this room setup in advance.

Depending on the placement of the projector cord, you might want to use duct tape to secure it to the floor and prevent a tripping hazard.

Before the session, ensure that the projector is focused so that the participants can see the entire image clearly. If you want to check the focus without revealing your images, place a coin with ridges (quarter or dime) on the glass and adjust the focus.

Keep the projector's surface clean because every bit of dirt and dust is magnified by about 100 times when it is projected on the screen.

The whirr of an overhead projector fan is often a bit noisy, so remember to project your voice and verify that everyone in the group can hear you.

Use a flat-sided implement, like a pencil, for a pointer because it will enable you to cleanly point out certain parts of the image and will not roll off the flat surface of the projector when you lay it down.

Use the "revelation" technique to reveal each point on the transparency one at a time by placing a piece of paper under the transparency. (If you put it on top of the transparency, it will slip off the moment you take your fingers away from it.)

Some additional facilitation tips when using transparencies and a projector include:

- Talk to the group—not the projector.
- Know how to turn off the projector and do so when changing transparencies (or you will blind the audience) or whenever you are not using a transparency as a visual aid.
- To prolong the life of the projector bulb and to prevent it from breaking due to the heat generated, run the fan for a few minutes after turning off the lamp.
- Either carry an emergency bulb with you or know how to contact the audiovisual technician at the meeting location in case the projector bulb burns out. A spare bulb is often stored in a compartment inside the projector itself.

Advantages of Using Overhead Transparencies

As a guideline, use overhead transparencies when:

- **Your budget is small or time is short**—transparencies can be made easily and are less expensive than slides.
- **You want to project existing materials to a group**—some transparencies are compatible with inkjet or laser printers. For example, you can print examples for forms, organizational charts, or graphics from your computer directly onto a transparency. Other transparencies can be

10 Rules to Follow When Creating Overhead Transparencies

Consider these things when creating overhead transparencies:

1. More is not always better. Keep the information on the transparency to a maximum of six lines with eight words per line per transparency.
2. If making transparencies from a computer printer or a photocopier, remember to make the size of the text large enough for the audience to easily see. Choose a clear and easy-to-ready typeface that has a font size of at least 24 points.
3. When choosing colors, apply the same principles as those outlined for flipcharts.
4. Use headings on each page to distinguish between key points and use bulleted lists to denote supporting points.
5. Be consistent with the font, colors, and formatting of headings, key points, and supporting points.
6. Keep some transparency markers in your toolkit because all markers are not created equal. Test them before the meeting.
7. Number each transparency on the border as well as on the actual transparency. You'll be glad you did if you drop them!
8. Write a corresponding number on each transparency to correspond with your notes so that you can seamlessly transition from one visual aid to another during your speech.
9. Always check your spelling.
10. If you are going to hand write the transparencies, make sure that your handwriting is legible. If not, consider making the transparencies by printing them from a computer or use presentation software.

STEP 5

loaded right into photocopiers so that you can create transparencies of anything that you can copy (for example, pages out of a book).

◆ **You want to capture ideas and solutions on the fly—** grease pencils and transparency markers enable you to write or emphasize a point during the session.

When Not to Use Overhead Transparencies

As a general rule, avoid using overhead transparencies when the meeting location is too small to contain a projector, a screen, and the audience—overhead projectors can be quite bulky and at times interfere with participants' line of sight.

PowerPoint or Other Presentation Software

PowerPoint and other types of software presentation tools have become so prevalent that they deserve discussion in their own visual aid category. Although overhead projectors and transparencies were once a staple of facilitation sessions and meetings, today presentation software now reigns as a key communication aid in many organizations.

Presentation software enables you to create digital slides that can be shown to an audience in a number of ways including

◆ a tabletop computer or liquid crystal diode (LCD) display on a laptop computer—use this for small groups

◆ a digital projector that interfaces directly with a laptop or personal digital assistant (PDA, special accessory required)

◆ a computer projector that sends images directly from your monitor onto a screen or flat surface—this is used for larger groups

◆ an overhead projector that uses specially made transparencies

◆ over the Internet or an organization's intranet

◆ hard copies of slides that can be distributed as handouts.

Presentation software offers many advantages over transitional visual aids, for example, its ease of use and the ability to capture "facilitator's notes" on each slide so that you can either print your "key points," which shows the slide image and your speaking notes, or display your speaking notes on the slide—which is only visible to you during the meeting.

Advantages of Using Presentation Software

As a guideline, use presentation software when:

- **Your meeting is formal**—presentation software tools are not only easy to use, but they also enable you to produce high-quality, professional-looking presentations.

- **You need flexibility to modify the meeting materials**—presentation software enables you to quickly add or replace slides using your keyboard. This means that you can easily tweak the topics and agenda and rearrange the flow of activities to be flexible and support the group's priorities.

- **Appropriate for audiences of all sizes**—materials created using this tool are professional looking and are just as appropriate for one or two people sitting around a table or a presentation for executives, to large groups in a conference center.

- **You want to reveal information in a specific manner**—when conducting a facilitation session, presentation software is especially adept at helping you to "reveal" the information that you want—when you want—to help guide the group through a logical problem-identification and decision-making process. Presentation software

POINTER

Assemble a facilitator's toolkit with the basics you'll need to facilitate the session in case the meeting room is not set up as you anticipated. Carry your own markers, sticky notes, index cards, and so on—whatever you will need for the session.

STEP **5**

10 Rules to Follow When Creating Materials Using Presentation Software

Here are 10 rules to apply when using presentation software:

1. Keep the design clean.
2. Don't add too many effects.
3. Keep the background subtle.
4. Use clip art sparingly.
5. Use the right graph style for the data.
6. Limit colors to three per slide.
7. Adhere to the six-by-six format: No more than six words per line and no more than six lines per slide.
8. Use light colors on dark backgrounds.
9. Keep sound and music clips brief.
10. Always practice the facilitation session flow in advance by projecting the materials to check for projection quality.

includes "builds" where you can display all topics or points to discuss on a slide, or with the click of your mouse or keyboard—you can reveal only the current topic at hand. This feature even "dims" the previous topics to help orient the audience not only to where they have been, but also to the current topic of discussion in case they "take a mental holiday" during the meeting.

When Not to Use Presentation Software

With all of the advantages of presentation software is there ever a time when you should not use this tool for facilitation sessions? As a general rule, do not use presentation software when:

◆ **You're fearful of new technology**—if you have a "technology phobia," you might want to avoid using presentation software unless you have adequate time to practice using the tool. If you are not comfortable using the technology, you might be distracted by trying to press the right button to advance slides rather than confidently facilitating the session.

Slides—Photographic or Digital

Millions of projector and photographic slides are used in the presentation world that can be projected directly from a laptop using PowerPoint or other presentation software. Whether the slides are photographic or digital—the guidelines are the same.

Advantages of Using Slides

As a guideline, use slides when:

◆ **Your presentation is formal**—making slides is not much of a technical issue, especially if you have access to a digital projector and presentation software.

◆ **The image conveys understanding**—a picture is often worth a thousand words, so use slides when a visual aid will readily help the group to comprehend information or clarify key points.

When Not to Use Slides

Because slides, like other visual aids, are not a one-size-fits-all solution, avoid using slides when:

◆ **A simpler solution will do**—why go to the trouble of making slides when a flipchart or quick presentation software solution would be just as effective?

◆ **You want to make changes to the material on the fly**—flipcharts and overhead transparencies enable you to make quick changes on the fly. If you are using traditional slides, revisions can be costly in terms of time and money.

Videotapes and DVDs

Using informational videotapes and DVDs can be an effective part of a facilitation session as a means of getting across a concept, providing background information, or simply offering some entertainment or a catalyst for discussion.

Using Videotapes and DVDs

When requesting and checking the meeting location setup, make sure that the proper equipment is available, works, and you know how to use it. Nothing is more embarrassing than having to apologize for equipment failures or your lack of expertise.

Depending on the size of the room and the audience, make sure that there are enough monitors throughout the room so that the entire group can see. Usually a minimum of a 25-inch monitor strategically placed will do the trick. The session will come to a halt if participants are craning their necks to see a videotape on a table at the front of the room.

Plan to show only short segments of the video—no more than 10 to 15 minutes each—before stopping the video and discussing the content.

Advantages of Videotapes and DVDs

As a guideline, use videotapes or DVDs when you want to dramatically illustrate a point or you want to entertain as well as inform the participants. These visual aids are particularly effective for demonstrating desired skills and behavior, process, and so on.

When Not to Use Videotapes and DVDs

As is true for any visual aid, proper use needs to always be top of mind. Do not use videotapes or DVDs when:

- ◆ **Your time is limited**—videos often stimulate discussion. The content will not be very valuable if you do not have time to discuss it.
- ◆ **You want to update or change your message**—changes to a video are expensive and can be very tricky.

Handouts

Handouts usually consist of either additional information related to the facilitation session or are the hard copies of the agenda, worksheets, and so on. Handouts are important for a number of reasons:

- They free participants to listen and actively discuss information rather than frantically taking notes.
- They enable you to provide additional information to participants that you might not be able to fully cover due to time constraints.
- They enable participants to personalize the materials by taking notes, highlighting important information, and jotting down ideas to share with the group.

Using Handouts

As with any other visual aid you use, handouts need to look professional. Be careful not to use too many different font styles and proof the pages to ensure that there are no misspellings. Staple or paperclip the handouts if they have multiple pages to make them easier to distribute and to ensure that participants receive all the pages.

Props

Presenters often overlook props as a visual aid—and only your imagination limits the type of props that you can use.

For example, one presenter took a basketball in one hand and a baseball in the other as he described the differences in weight of two issues he was discussing.

Introducing anything like props into your meeting also takes a little courage. After all, the approach might resonate with participants or they might not quite understand the symbolism. Try out your props when doing a run-through of your facilitation plan with friends or colleagues.

You now have a solid understanding of the variety of media choices available to enhance your facilitation session. Use Worksheet 5.1 to make sure you have selected the right technology for your needs.

Next Steps to Take

With your media selected, the next step in becoming a master facilitator includes preparing to facilitate a session. Because adults all learn and process information differently, successful facilitators possess a solid understanding of adult learning styles and preferences, and how they affect facilitation discussions. The next chapter will arm you with all of this information as well as provide practical tips for practicing and honing your skills to become a successful facilitator.

WORKSHEET 5.1
Media and Technology Planning Checklist

Use this checklist to ensure that you have considered all media implications when preparing to facilitate a meeting.

The media selected . . .

☐ Incorporates the appropriate amount of movement for facilitator and participant activities.

☐ Maintains an appropriate level of formality/informality.

☐ Provides an appropriate level of intellectual interactivity.

☐ Offers an appropriate level of physical interactivity.

☐ Includes an appropriate level of activity for the time of day.

☐ Involves an appropriate amount of light in the room for the time of day.

☐ Is the correct medium for variability and evolution of the session agenda and facilitation processes.

☐ Is portable and can be modified on the fly, if needed.

You've prepared for facilitating using media by . . .

☐ Incorporating a variety of media into the session.

☐ Assessing the physical environment and mating the best media to the environment.

☐ Planning for backup media, just in case.

☐ Obtaining permission for material obtained (for example, copyright approvals, if necessary).

NOTES

_____

_____

_____

_____

_____

_____

_____

_____

_____

_____

_____

_____

_____

_____

_____

_____

_____

_____

_____

_____

_____

_____

_____

_____

_____

_____

_____

_____

Prepare to Facilitate

Learning styles and how people take in information

Learning styles: How adults process information

Practice, practice, practice

Rehearsing the facilitation session flow

Tools and techniques to avoid jitters

Successful facilitators understand that people learn and take in information in different ways: visually, auditorily, and kinesthetically. To accommodate the various needs of participants, facilitators need to consider how to help everyone in the group understand the issues or discussions clearly. For example, some participants absorb information easiest if they are provided with visuals such as an agenda, a list of issues, a matrix for making decisions, and so on. Other participants comprehend what's going on best by listening to discussions and debating key points. And still another group of participants must be doing something with their hands or moving around to get the creative juices flowing to contribute most to the session.

So how do facilitators cater to all of the different ways that participants prefer to take in and process information? They consider a variety of approaches when preparing to facilitate a session.

Learning Styles and How People Prefer to Take in Information

You're probably familiar with the findings that, "Adults retain about 10 percent of what they read, 20 percent of what they hear,

30 percent of what they see, and 50 percent of what they hear and see. But, if adults become actively involved those percentages rise to 70 percent of what they say and 90 percent of what they both say and do" (cited in McCain and Tobey, 2004, p. 23).

The most successful facilitators become experts in a variety of instructional and facilitative methods—and tailor them to the learning styles and needs of the participants. By meeting the needs of participants who prefer to take in information visually, aurally, or kinesthetically, facilitators can dramatically increase the learning experience and participation of the group.

The next section describes the unique characteristics of each type of learner and what types of visual aids or activities facilitators should include during the meeting.

Visual Learning Preference

Visual learners take in and process information through what they see. They learn best from printed information, pictures, graphics, and the like. Incorporating some of the following items into the facilitation session accommodates the visual learner's preferences:

- overhead transparencies
- flipcharts
- wallboards
- demonstrations
- diagrams, charts, and drawings
- participant materials such as agenda, meeting notes, lists of brainstormed ideas or identified issues
- videos.

Auditory Learning Preference

Auditory learners take in and process information that is heard, including words, alliterations, and songs. To aid the learner with an auditory preference, consider incorporating

- presentations
- facilitative discussions

- demonstrations
- group work and activities with feedback
- verbal instructions
- audiovisuals
- songs
- background instrumental music
- panel discussions
- question–and–answer sessions.

Kinesthetic Learning Preference

Kinesthetic, or physical, learners take in and process information through physical experiences. They like direct involvement and physical activity. To aid participants with a kinesthetic learning preference, consider incorporating

- hands-on work, including creating lists, brainstorming, and working with flipcharts and other media
- role plays
- structured note-taking (where participants fill out worksheets and documents based on the discussions in the facilitation session)
- individual and group activities and projects
- creating their own materials such as drawings, flipcharts, and posters.

So how do facilitators accomplish all of these items? Although a facilitator needs to lead discussions and

STEP 6

POINTER

Begin and end all meetings on time. Late-coming participants will quickly learn that you do not hold the meeting for stragglers and everyone will appreciate ending at the appointed time.

present information at times, facilitative discussions allow others to voice their views and experiences (auditory learning experience). When facilitators use multiple forms of media, they meet the needs of visual learners. When facilitators have groups work in teams to generate ideas and flipchart them, then kinesthetic learners are fully engaged. The challenge for facilitators is to incorporate as many of these options as possible into the session simultaneously.

Learning Styles: How Adults Process Information

Now that you have an understanding of how learners prefer to take in information (learning preferences), you can move on to how learners process that information. The different ways that people process information are called learning styles. Five distinct learning styles have been identified:

- ◆ achievers
- ◆ evaluators
- ◆ networkers
- ◆ socializers
- ◆ observers.

Achievers

Achievers focus on accomplishing results and generally have the expertise to do so. People with this learning style are good at finding practical uses for ideas and theories. They enjoy being involved in new and challenging experiences and carrying out plans to meet those challenges. Achievers have the ability to solve problems, make decisions, and develop action plans based on implementing solutions to questions or problems. They want to find practical uses for ideas. Achievers like to accept the lead role in addressing those challenges.

Achievers thrive on sequence and logical order and clear, step-by-step directions. They do not have strong social skills and have a tendency to take control with little regard for others' feelings.

Because achievers are "take charge" people, consider rotating small group leadership roles to ensure all participants have a chance. With achievers, the facilitator needs to be practical and help the group to derive solutions for what will really work back on the job.

In small-group work the achiever may monopolize the conversation, dictate the direction and solution, and show little respect or patience for others' opinions or experience. They want activity directions stated logically (preferably in writing) with specific outcomes identified. If needed, revisit the agreed-upon ground rules concerning everyone's participation, the value of others' opinions, and mutual respect.

Evaluators

Sometimes referred to as thinkers, evaluators like to analyze a situation and use a logical process to resolve issues. They ask many detailed questions and in doing so collect a great deal of information. They are very concerned about working within the existing guidelines. Evaluators are good at assimilating a wide range of information and putting it into concise, logical form, using lists, charts, or planning tools. These learners are more interested in the basis or theory and application of theory and less on building relationships. The information and theory discussed in the facilitation session needs to be logically sound, exact, and supported by facts.

POINTER

Plan a variety of activities and visual aids that accommodate all participants' learning styles and preferences.

STEP 6

Evaluators need to see value and job-relatedness of the facilitation session discussion and activities. They want to set up an orderly way (logical steps) to address the purpose of the activity. Be aware, though, that the evaluator may challenge the expertise of the achiever and others.

Networkers

These learners like to develop close relationships with others and avoid interpersonal conflict. Because they are good listeners, they develop strong networks of people. They are more compliant than others and are often easily swayed. Networkers try to avoid risks, seek consensus, and are slower than others to make decisions. In group activities, networkers rarely disagree with others' opinions, but rather are supportive of others and seek collaboration. Networkers take time to build trust and get personally acquainted with others. Although they are outgoing, they need direct feedback to get support.

Socializers

These learners like to talk and share. They enjoy the spotlight and like to have fun. Although they value multiple perspectives, they are good at selling their ideas to others and building alliances. Socializers are not concerned with details or facts. They move at a fast pace and make quick, spontaneous decisions. In group work, the socializer wants to work quickly, seek others' input, persuade others, get the job done quickly, provide some humor, and volunteer to make presentations (for example, they will report ideas generated or summarize the thoughts of a group after breakout activities, and so on).

Socializers like presentations of group activities and must be reminded that a presentation requires depth; superficial responses are not enough. To accomplish this, ask socializers for their rationale or for the facts behind their comments. Strive to take them deeper into the content. In large-group discussions, recognize their contributions but ask for alternative views. Socializers are good at brainstorming activities.

Observers

These learners are best at considering concrete situations from many different points of view. They prefer to observe and conceptualize rather than take action. They are reflective thinkers. They enjoy situations that call for generating not just many ideas, but a wide range of ideas. These learners are more interested in abstract ideas and concepts and less in building relationships. Observers want to take time to reflect and conceptualize, and they do not like to wing it.

When creating a learning experience, involve observers and let them reflect on in what they have experienced. Debriefing of activities could take the form of building on the results and going into more abstract ideas, such as generating future situations.

As a facilitator, you'll want to recognize the five different learning styles and address all the learners' needs. A quick way to tentatively identify these styles is through the learners' choice of words and behaviors. Table 6.1 provides a brief summary of verbal cues and learner behavior to help you recognize these styles.

POINTER

Plan activities that get participants out of their chairs to get them up and moving. If space is limited and it is not practical for people to mill around the room or in breakout rooms, include "toys" in the middle of the tables to keep kinesthetic learners engaged. Koosh or squeeze balls, pipe cleaners, and so forth that do not make noise when played with will keep idle energy in check and participants focused.

STEP 6

TABLE 6.1
Recognizing Learning Styles

Role	Verbal Cue	Behavior
Achiever	Tells, does little asking Blunt, to the point Asks for clear directions Asks for clear, concise answers Asks about how to apply on the job	Does lots of talking Takes charge, likes to be leader Follows handouts and directions in order Demonstrates little patience for nontask-related activities
Evaluator	Asks for data, facts, sources Focuses comments on the topic Little personal sharing Wants the details	Task oriented Follows directions Challenges others' expertise Develops steps to accomplish activities
Networker	Asks many questions Does little telling Vocalizes support for others' opinions Seeks attention and feedback	Engages in effective listening Seeks collaboration and consensus Reserves personal opinions Avoids conflict Develops close relationships Builds trust
Socializer	Shares experiences Tells stories Digresses and gets off the subject Readily expresses personal opinion Talks a lot Uses language of persuasion	Makes quick, spontaneous decisions without all the information Gets multiple perspectives Has fun Loves group activities and discussions
Observer	Likes to conceptualize, "what if" discussions Asks questions or makes comments off the direct subject Makes "what about this" statements Applies information learned to future discussions	Provides several alternatives to a problem or situation Easily gets off the subject Wants further discussion on the idea Not concerned with the concrete application of ideas

STEP 6

Now that you know about learner preferences for taking in content and learner styles for processing information, you, as a facilitator, will want to use both sets of information in making a conscious decision regarding meeting the needs of the facilitation session participants. Worksheet 6.1 integrates learning preferences and styles with various facilitation activity choices to help you align activities with learning preferences and styles.

Meeting the Needs of Different Learning Preferences

Although we discussed how different types of learners prefer to take in and process information, keep in mind that people with different styles and preferences engage differently—which means that facilitators must carefully weigh and decide on the type of facilitation activities to include. Three guidelines to help in addressing learning preferences and styles include:

1. **Two out of three, every time:** Use techniques that appeal to at least two of the three learning preferences in every activity. For example, if you provide instructions for an activity verbally and put them on a flipchart or a handout, you have hit the auditory and visual preferences at the same time. In many cases, you can hit all three preferences.

2. **Change up often:** By transitioning to a new topic or activity (or both) often and by changing the type of activity, you'll hit different combinations of preferences and styles throughout the meeting. You can also vary the session by altering the pace and sequencing of topics.

3. **Watch out for your own style:** The activities you are most comfortable facilitating are most likely the ones that match your own learning style. If you're not careful, you'll tend to use those activities too much. Effective facilitators take themselves out of their own comfort zones and choose to facilitate all kinds of learning activities so that all kinds of learning styles are accommodated.

Practice, Practice, Practice

When preparing to facilitate a meeting, be prepared! There are several things you can do prior to facilitating a session to help you anticipate and prepare for the unexpected.

Practice provides an opportunity to polish and rethink structure, as well as to remember the flow and activities that comprise the session. The time spent practicing is usually proportional to the level of relaxation you experience the day of the facilitation session. Knowing the flow of events and how to facilitate the activities appropriately is a direct result of the time you spend practicing and preparing.

A key to practicing is to rehearse what you are going to say at the opening of the meeting. Memorize the first few paragraphs. Usually having the introduction memorized or thoroughly practiced will reduce your stress level and get the facilitation session started on the right foot.

Throughout the facilitation session, aim to be
- honest
- accurate
- clear
- informative
- interesting.

STEP 6

POINTER

Throughout the facilitation session, aim to be honest, accurate, clear, informative, and interesting.

Notice that "entertaining" is not on the list. Remember, a facilitation session is not about you—it's about the participants and helping the group to achieve the desired outcomes. As a result, keep in mind the various techniques used to involve the group.

Rehearsing the Facilitation Session Flow

The first 90 seconds of a facilitation session are important because they set the tone for the rest of the meeting. If you start off on the right foot, chances are you'll continue along that path. If, however, you start off on the wrong foot, it can be very difficult to recover. That's why great facilitators have the first 90 seconds of their opening down pat. Once again, it's all about being prepared. When you start strong, the group becomes energized and engaged.

Once you know what you're going to say, consider some of these suggestions for that first 90 seconds:

- Look like you're confident even if your knees are shaking.
- Acknowledge the group, smile (if appropriate), and start talking.
- Exhibit an outward appearance that says to the participants that there isn't any other place you'd rather be.
- Begin by painting a mental picture with your words and actions for the group right from the start.
- Be focused, positive, and enthusiastic, and speak confidently.

Remember, the qualities that successful facilitators demonstrate during facilitation sessions include

- respect for self and for listeners
- honesty
- objectivity
- sense of humor
- adequate preparation
- balanced confidence and modesty
- verbal, vocal, and physical communication skills
- appropriate appearance.

Tools and Techniques to Avoid the Jitters

Nothing helps you to overcome nervousness better than knowing your facilitation plan and how to help the

POINTER

Plan what you are going to say for the first 90 seconds of the facilitation session opening. The opening sets the tone for the rest of the meeting. Chances are, if you start off on the right foot, you'll continue down that path for the rest of the meeting.

STEP 6

group accomplish the defined outcomes. To accomplish this goal, consider some of these techniques to practice your plan before a facilitation session.

- **Practice in front of a mirror**—some facilitators find this technique helpful, but it may subtly reinforce the notion that you're talking to and for yourself rather than the group.
- **Video camera**—this tool gives you an opportunity to observe your body language as well as hear yourself; however, like listening to yourself on a tape recorder, a video camera may discourage you when reviewing the tape of your facilitation skills.
- **Friendly critic**—this technique puts the emphasis on projecting to a group. Be sure that the critic understands what you are trying to do and what his or her role is in providing you with feedback or reacting to the facilitation plan and flow.
- **Focus on nonverbal aspects**—although most facilitators practice what they plan to say, don't forget to practice making eye contact (looking away from your notes and the facilitation plan at different points around the room) and using hand gestures, voice inflection, and your body language in general.
- **Dress rehearsal**—find out if you can schedule time to practice or have a dress rehearsal in the room where the facilitation session will take place. Even if you cannot rehearse in the meeting location, be sure to practice with visuals, handouts, and all materials that you need to synchronize with the facilitation session flow and discussion. This is especially true if you plan to use various types of media.

With your facilitation techniques in mind, the next step in the process to becoming a successful facilitator includes understanding how groups develop and identifying and managing difficult participants.

WORKSHEET 6.1

Aligning Activities with Learning Preferences and Styles

Use this worksheet to integrate learning preferences and styles with various facilitation activities to help you align activities with the learning preferences and styles of the group members.

Learning Activity	Visual Preference	Auditory Preference	Kinesthetic Preference	Achiever Style	Evaluator Style	Networker Style	Socializer Style	Observer Style
Lecture		X		X	X			
Handouts	X			X	X			X
Group Discussion		X				X	X	X
Role Play			X	X	X		X	X[1]
Group Work at Flipchart	X	X	X			X	X	X
Case Study		X		X	X			X

(continued on next page)

STEP 6

Learning Activity	Visual Preference	Auditory Preference	Kinesthetic Preference	Achiever Style	Evaluator Style	Networker Style	Socializer Style	Observer Style
Hands-on Practice			X	X				
Note-taking	X		X		X			X
Games	X	X	X	X		X	X	
Small-Group Work		X		X[2]		X	X	X[3]
Activity Debriefing		X		X	X			X
Action Planning			X	X	X	X		X
Brainstorming		X		X		X	X	

[1]If they observe and don't participate in the action.
[2]If they have a leadership role.
[3]If opportunity is given to comment on observations during activity.

STEP 6

Leverage Strategies to Deal with Group Conflict and Difficult Participants

OVERVIEW

Strategies for dealing with group conflict

Stages of team development

Identifying behaviors that enhance or hinder effectiveness

Any time a work group is formed, the individuals involved bring their own preconceived thoughts and beliefs to the table. Depending on the organization, there may be additional group dynamics at work such as norms and organizational culture. The size of the group, whether it is formal or informal, and the type of leadership also affect the group.

To facilitate efficiently, facilitators need to know enough about the group to guide and model effective processes.

Strategies for Dealing with Group Conflict and Difficult Participants

Effective groups don't just happen. Often a group's success is predicated on a successful facilitator whose primary responsibilities are

Establish ground rules. Ground rules detail the standards of behavior that the group expects of each participant. The group should develop the ground rules—and can add to them as needed. The facilitator's role is to enforce the ground rules, but often the group self-polices one other.

to guide the group toward successful decision making. An effective facilitator can maximize group participation, productivity, and satisfaction.

Because a facilitator's focus is on managing the decision-making process, he or she needs to have a solid understanding of people, groups, facilitating styles, and the stages of group development.

Stages of Team Development

Teams or groups often generate a tremendous amount of positive energy when they are first formed. Members are excited, motivated, and ready to roll up their sleeves and tackle tasks immediately. As individuals join together, the group takes on a new life of its own. It will even go through stages of development comparable to the stages of individual growth: infancy, childhood, adolescence, adulthood, and old age. Each stage has its own characteristics and requirements and each builds on the preceding phases.

Although the stages of development are sequentially predictable, each group is unique in how it progresses and regresses through these stages. Some phases can be more painful than others; sometimes groups get stuck in a particular stage and cannot advance.

Although numerous classifications of group-development stages exist, Bruce Tuckman and Mary Jane Jensen have identified five stages that capture group-development strategies for dealing with group conflict, they are:

1. forming
2. storming
3. norming
4. performing
5. adjourning.

Forming

During this stage, group members tend to be extremely polite. They seek guidance and may be reluctant to participate. Serious topics and expression of personal feelings are avoided. At this stage, the group needs to get acquainted and share personal information. Members should explore the similarities they share and orient themselves toward the task they've been assigned to address. To grow from this stage to the next, group members must be willing to confront threatening topics and risk the possibility of conflict.

Facilitators can support forming by

- planning introductions and orientation
- reviewing the agenda and stating the desired outcomes
- using warm-up activities
- soliciting and listening to expectations from the participants
- establishing ground rules
- agreeing on decision-making methods.

Storming

As groups move from the forming stage, they may ask questions such as:

STEP 7

- Who is responsible for what?
- What are the rules?
- What are the "hidden agendas?"
- Are there "invisible committees?"

During this stage, boundaries are tested and power struggles or conflicts may develop. Cliques may form. Some members may remain silent, whereas others attempt to dominate. To grow from this stage to the next, group members must be willing to give up personal preferences in favor of the requirements of the total group. The group members need to listen, be nondefensive, confront others in a positive way, and be willing to influence and be influenced. Keep in mind that not every conflict is an indication of storming—conflict can be healthy!

At this point in the process, facilitators can help guide the group through this stage by addressing the storming issues of the group, modeling appropriate behavior, and promoting good conflict-resolution processes, including

- separating problems from the individuals
- not taking storming issues personally
- enforcing ground rules and their role as the process expert.

Norming

When groups move from storming to norming, they begin merging into a cohesive group (there is more cooperation and understanding). The group has negotiated roles, successfully manages differences of opinion, develops both written and unwritten rules or norms, recognizes the need for interdependence, and masters decision-making mechanics. The group is now ready to tackle the task.

Unfortunately, many groups do not make it to this stage. If a group has not established positive relationships during its early stages, or if conflict remains unresolved, these factors will impede the group's ability to make effective decisions.

At this point in the group development process, the facilitator should

- observe emerging norms
- encourage the value of expressing differences positively and working toward group cohesiveness
- facilitate negotiation.

Performing

The move from the norming to the performing stage is characterized by a high level of trust. Members are recognized for, and encouraged to use, their unique talents. Paradoxically, when a group is highly cohesive and long lived, it is also susceptive to "group think." Group think occurs when individual members suppress their objections and criticisms of others' ideas so that the group can reach agreement with minimal conflict. As a result, the group will make riskier, less-thoughtful decisions.

Facilitators should support the group by

- guiding the group through effective processes to accomplish the desired outcomes
- avoiding the temptation to intervene unless the group is truly stuck and floundering.

Adjourning

During this last stage, the group prepares for termination. Groups may disband because their work is completed or because group members no longer feel challenged by the task.

To aid groups through these developmental stages, effective facilitators should be able to

- establish a climate that encourages and recognizes participation
- listen intently, synthesize, and restate various viewpoints
- "take the group's pulse"—understand and recognize where they are and where they need to be
- describe what is going on and what is unspoken

◆ find areas of agreement and common threads

◆ design and apply a variety of techniques and processes to encourage creativity and productivity

◆ be flexible.

Identifying Behaviors that Enhance or Hinder Group Effectiveness

So how do facilitators watch groups in action and figure out exactly what participants are doing that either reduces or increases the group's effectiveness? Successful facilitators follow these steps:

◆ Step 1: Observe behaviors

◆ Step 2: Interpret meaning from the behavior

◆ Step 3: Determine whether it is appropriate to intervene or not

◆ Step 4: Describe the behavior and provide feedback.

Step 1: The Power of Observation

All interventions have one thing in common: the facilitator provides proper feedback and times the intervention to alter what the group is doing. This means that the facilitator must pay careful attention to group activity, as well as the interactions among individual group members.

The ground rules established at the start of the facilitation session outline one set of agreed-upon behaviors expected by the group. Therefore, participants displaying behavior counter to those ground rules are most likely showing ineffective behavior.

Facilitators need to possess knowledge in two areas: 1) the type of behavior to look for and 2) how an effective group functions.

Listening Skills

When facilitators observe, they are using a methodical approach. A key skill needed when observing groups includes listening to what's going on, what is being said, and how it is conveyed.

Listening shows interest in the individual who is speaking and respect for others' experience. Three types of listening include:

- ◆ **Passive listening**—in which there is no interaction possible, such as listening to the radio or television.
- ◆ **Attentive listening**—where some interaction is possible with the speaker—such as listening to a lecture in a class or taking notes in a meeting.
- ◆ **Active listening**—in which participants have a high level of interaction with the speaker and listen for content, meaning, and feelings.

Facilitators listen actively throughout the meeting. They observe who spoke, exactly what was said verbatim, how long the person spoke, whom individuals look at when they speak, who supports whom, any challenges to group leadership, nonverbal communication, side conversations, and nonparticipation. They wait for individual reactions to what is being said to help guide and coach the group. Facilitators may ask questions, restate what has been said, summarize positions, or reflect a speaker's feelings. They may also keep track of the different roles group members play.

Step 2: Interpreting Meaning from Group and Individual Behaviors

STEP 7

Many facilitators find it helpful to develop a chart to "keep score" of the group members' different behaviors. Although charting is a helpful technique, facilitators should get the group's permission to use it—especially in the early stages when participants may not completely trust each other. You may want to use Worksheet 7.1 to track the behaviors of the group you are facilitating.

The chart attempts to quantify the contributions of group members in two broad categories: task and maintenance:

- ◆ **Task functions**—facilitate the group in selecting, defining, and solving a common problem.

WORKSHEET 7.1
Tracking Group and Individual Behaviors

Many facilitators use checklists to track the behaviors—both good and bad—of group members. This allows the facilitator to provide accurate feedback at the end of a meeting. Keeping track of behaviors can make criticism and feedback specific, objective, and therefore, easier to take. And it helps to know everyone in the group is receiving the same type of commentary.

Keep in mind that checklists may make group members uncomfortable. When using this tool, be sure to gain the group's approval and agreement on how the data will be used and discussed.

Notice the column headings for group members' names. Facilitators may want to designate one column for tracking general "group" behavior. During the session, tally how many times an individual or the group engages in a particular behavior. For example, group members may feel that, as a group, they interrupt each other too much. The facilitator may be asked to note that one aspect and report to the team at the end of the meeting. Facilitators can also use the tallies on this worksheet as a confidence-builder by tracking various desirable leadership behaviors and report back on them.

Behaviors	Members								
Task Activity									
Initiator									
Information seeker									
Clarifier									
Summarizer									
Consensus tester									
Information giver									

STEP 7

Worksheet 7.1, continued

Behaviors	Members								
Maintenance Activity									
Encourager									
Expresser of group feelings									
Harmonizer									
Compromiser									
Gatekeeper									
Standard setter									
Coach									
Collaborator									
Individual Activity									
Blocker									
Avoider									
Digressor									
Recognition seeker									
Dominator									

STEP 7

◆ **Maintenance functions**—alter or maintain the way in which group members interact.

The chart also records any antigroup roles adopted by individuals. Table 7.1 lists and describes some of the group's behaviors that facilitators may want to chart.

Other areas that facilitators observe that may help groups function more efficiently include

- ◆ group rules
- ◆ idea clarification
- ◆ handling group problems
- ◆ favoritism
- ◆ group status
- ◆ sensitivity to needs of the group
- ◆ positive or negative body language
- ◆ seating arrangements
- ◆ tension
- ◆ program planning
- ◆ hidden agendas
- ◆ invisible committees
- ◆ making others aware of their own contributions.

Step 3: Determine Whether and When to Intervene

The word "intervention" is derived from the Latin word meaning to "interfere with the affairs of others." Facilitators use interventions to shift the focus of a process or to engage passive participants. Four types of interventions include

- ◆ interventions that cause the group to examine its dynamics and improve its performance

TABLE 7.1

Summary of Task, Maintenance, and Individual Behaviors

Functions	Behavior	Definition
Task Activity	Initiating	Proposing tasks or goals, defining the problem, suggesting a procedure or ideas for solving the problem.
	Information seeking	Requesting facts, seeking relevant data about a problem, asking for suggestions or ideas.
	Clarifying	Clearing up confusion, indicating alternatives and issues, giving examples.
	Summarizing	Restating suggestions, synthesizing ideas, offering a decision or direction for the group to accept or reject.
	Consensus testing	Setting up straw men to see if the group is near conclusion, checking to see how much agreement has been reached.
Maintenance Activity	Encouraging	Being friendly, recognizing others.
	Expressing group feelings	Sensing moods, feelings, relationships with others, sharing feelings.
	Harmonizing	Reconciling disagreements, reducing tensions, getting others to explore their differences.
	Compromising	Admitting error, disciplining oneself to maintain group cohesion.
	Gatekeeping	Trying to keep communication channels open, suggesting procedures or inducing discussions of group problems.
	Setting standards	Expressing standards to achieve, applying standards to evaluate the group and its output, evaluating frequently.
	Coaching and consulting	Working with group members and management outside of the meeting.

STEP 7

(continued on next page)

Table 7.1, continued

Functions	Behavior	Definition
Individual Activity	Blocking	Interfering with group progress by arguing, resisting, disagreeing, or beating a dead horse.
	Avoiding	Withdrawing from the discussion, daydreaming, doing something else, whispering, leaving the room.
	Digressing	Going off the subject, filibustering, discussing personal issues.

◆ interventions that encourage member participation

◆ interventions that encourage problem solving and decision making

◆ interventions that ensure compliance with procedures, policies, ground rules, and requirements that define the process within the organization.

Active interventions alter the flow of events. They may quicken the development of the group, change the course of the discussion, increase the group's energy, or help the group become more aware of how it is functioning.

Facilitators should not intervene unless there is reason to—that is, the intervention should alter what the group is doing or make available some additional information. Facilitators should intervene when the group wanders off track, when two participants are in conflict, when an individual isn't participating or is angry, or when a participant becomes autocratic.

Timing is everything—and depending on what is occurring, facilitators may choose to intervene before, during, or after the meeting.

How to Intervene

Knowing how to intervene is a required skill of successful facilitators. Consider these guidelines on how to intervene in a group's process:

- **Describe process obstacles**—if nothing is happening, describe the next step and perhaps encourage the contributions of several participants.

- **Encourage participation**—at the start of the meeting and plan activities to maintain that participation throughout the session.

- **Use body language**—by moving closer to the table or particular participants to either support those who are under fire or to quiet down disruptive members.

- **Discourage personal attacks**—by reminding individuals and the group of the ground rules and refocus the discussion on the issue to dissuade personal attacks.

- **Suggest a break**—to end a deadlock or simply reenergize the group. Refreshment breaks are common, but others work just as well, such as moving to small breakout groups for a few minutes or taking a five-minute joke break.

- **Summarize**—any problem(s) and alternatives that the group generated. Groups may get lost in discussion and summarizing helps the group refocus and keep moving.

- **Have the group manage the process**—as the group matures. Turning over some facilitation duties indicates both trust and respect for the group and its interactions.

- **Debrief the group**—to examine what is happening. Debriefing requires all group members to reflect on the meeting and is usually done at the end of the session or may be useful at natural breaks in the meeting agenda.

- **Search for common threads**—if the group is wandering. Stop the meeting and ask for the group to search for what the solution or problem definitions have in common.

- **Present a straw man**—by developing (or suggesting that someone develop) a draft problem description or solution during a break. A straw man encourages the group to criticize the plan, attack it, pull it apart.

- **Act stupid**—to help participants who are uninvolved or may not understand what is happening or what someone is saying. These participants may not want to volunteer their

ignorance. Ask for clarification of issues, problems, termi-
nology, or anything else that may get in the way of consensus later in the process.

◆ **Get specific**—to help clear up hard-to-grasp issues, problems, and solutions.

Groups and
individual
participants will
exhibit behavior
that at times may
hinder the group.
As a facilitator, do
not take this
behavior personally!
Observe the group
and participant
behaviors and
intervene when
necessary to resolve
conflicts in a healthy
manner and to keep
the group on track.

Diagnosing and Managing Difficult Participants

Group members often take on behaviors
that hinder the group process. So why do
some people end up labeled as difficult
participants? Keep in mind that individuals in a group often have their own moti-
vations and agendas. For example, if a
participant challenges your expertise—as
a facilitator you must never take this behavior personally even though it may
seem like you are being attacked. How
you react to challenging individuals can
either enhance or undermine your credibility and either enhance or disrupt the
group processes. So handling difficult participant behavior effectively is mission
critical!

A facilitator's response to difficult behavior must be depersonalized. The deper-
sonalization process begins by making a
change in how you view difficult participants. Rather then label "them" difficult
participants, call it disruptive behavior. In
this way, you are labeling the behavior—not the people. Also, the
term "disruptive" is both less personal and more accurate in describing the effects of that behavior.

In dealing with disruptive behavior, your job is to set aside your personal agenda, which is, without fail, to guide the group through processes to help the group perform effectively and achieve the defined outcomes. More often than not, when you meet a participant's personal agenda, his or her agenda goes away and often the disruptive behavior is extinguished.

So, what happens if you take all of the appropriate steps to shut down disruptive behavior but it still continues? At that point, you have a dilemma. The science of group dynamics shows that when disruptive behavior is allowed to continue, sometimes the group itself will shut down the behavior. Some of the things the group may do in this regard include shunning the participant who is behaving disruptively, using negative nonverbal behaviors (for example, eye-rolling), ignoring and not responding to the participant's remarks, and carrying on side conversations when that participant is speaking. This is a more desirable scenario than you having to continue to deal with the behavior or having to shut it down yourself, but it doesn't always happen this way.

So, do you wait and hope the group will become so frustrated with the negative behavior that it shuts the person down? Do you continue to act on your professional agenda in dealing with the behavior and hope that the third time is the charm? Do you take the matter into your own hands and deal with the person in a more disciplinary manner?

STEP 7

It's your call. There will be times when your judgment must come into play, when you believe you need to act more leniently or more firmly than you'd like. Sooner or later you will experience the Catch-22 of facilitation: If you err on the side of leniency, the group will be disappointed and evaluations will say that you are "too nice." If you err on the side of firmness, you will receive negative evaluations that you are "too strict."

There will be times when your judgment as a facilitator is called into play—when you believe you must act more firmly or leniently than you would like. Don't let that dissuade you from intervening when the group or individual participants need guidance to get them back on track!

Table 7.2 presents and dissects many of the disruptive behaviors you might experience, explains why group members may behave that way, and provides suggestions for handling the disruptive behavior.

In general, facilitator tactics for handling disruptive behavior should include

- ◆ not getting caught in one-on-one power struggles
- ◆ using good-natured humor
- ◆ connecting with the participant on a personal level
- ◆ broadening the participation of the rest of the group
- ◆ protecting participants as needed
- ◆ using a separate "issues" chart or "parking lot" to postpone issues until they are appropriate for discussion
- ◆ recognizing the individual's point and then either gaining the viewpoints of others or taking the discussion offline
- ◆ modifying facilitation session activities or small-group compositions.

Step 4: Describing Behavior and Providing Feedback

When providing feedback regarding disruptive behaviors, you should be descriptive, specific, and mindful of the needs of the group—not individuals. You need to describe what you privately observed in step 1 that led you to intervene. Remember to always use the ground rules that the group agreed to when explaining

TABLE 7.2

Identifying and Handling Disruptive Behaviors

Behavior	Why It Happens	What to Do
Heckler	Is probably good natured most of the time but is distracted by job or personal problems	• Keep your temper under control. • Honestly agree with one idea, then move on to something else. • Toss a misstatement of fact to the group to turn down. • Talk privately with the person as a last resort to determine what is bothering him or her.
Rambler	One idea leads to another and takes this person miles away from the original point	• When there is a pause for breath, thank him or her, refocus attention, and move on. • In a friendly manner, indicate that "we are a little off subject." • As a last resort, use your agenda timetable. Glance at your watch and say, "Time is limited."
Ready Answer	Really wants to help, but makes it difficult by keeping others from participating	• Cut this off tactfully by questioning others. Suggest that "we put others to work." • Ask this person to summarize. It keeps him or her attentive and capitalizes on his or her enthusiasm.
Conversationalist	Side chatter is usually personal in nature but may be related to the topic.	• Call by name and ask an easy question. • Call by name, restate the last opinion expressed, and ask his or her opinion of it. • Include him or her in the discussion.

STEP 7

(continued on next page)

Table 7.2, continued

Behavior	Why It Happens	What to Do
Personality Problems	Two or more individuals clash, dividing the group into factions and endangering the success of the meeting.	• Maximize points of agreement; minimize disagreements. Draw attention to the objective at hand. • Pose a direct question to an uninvolved member on the topic. As a last resort, frankly state that personalities should be left out of the discussion.
Wrong Track	Brings up ideas that are obviously incorrect.	• Say, "That's one way of looking at it," and tactfully make any corrections or solicit someone else's opinion to help convey the correct information to the group. • Say, "I see your point, but can we reconcile that with our current situation?" • Handle tactfully because you will be contradicting him or her. Remember, all group members will hear how you respond to this individual. Your response will either encourage or discourage future participation.
Quiet One	Bored	• Gain interest by asking for opinion.
	Indifferent	• Question the person next to him or her. Then ask the quiet one to comment on the view expressed.
	Timid	• Compliment this person the first time he or she contributes. Be sincere.
	Superior	• Indicate respect for this person's experience, then ask for ideas.
Bungler	Lacks the ability to put good ideas into proper order; needs help to convey ideas.	• Don't call attention to the problem. Say, "Let me see if I am understanding what you are saying . . . " then repeat the idea more clearly.

Table 7.2, continued

Behavior	Why It Happens	What to Do
Mule	Can't or won't see the other side; supports own viewpoint no matter what.	• Ask other members of the group to comment on the ideas. They will straighten him or her out. • Remind him or her that time is short, and suggest that he or she accept the group consensus presently. Indicate your willingness to talk with him or her later. Then, follow up.
Talker	Highly motivated Show-off Well informed Just plain talkative	• Slow this person down with some difficult questions. • Say, "That's an interesting point. Now let's see what the rest think of it . . . " • Draw on his or her knowledge, but relay to the group. • In general, for all overly talkative folks, let the group take care of them as much as possible.
Griper	Has a pet peeve, gripes for the sake of complaining, or has a legitimate complaint.	• Point out that the objective at hand is to operate as efficiently and cooperatively as possible under the present circumstances. • Indicate that you will discuss his or her personal problem privately at a later date. • Have another member of the group respond to his or her complaint.

your observation and interpretation of the behavior. You are using the ground rules to test your assumptions—so this is not a personal attack, just a professional observation to try and help the group function more efficiently. At this point, test whether the group agrees with the observations.

Keep in mind that group members may see things differently! Ask the group whether you have accurately captured the exchange or behaviors. If you misheard something—and the group calls you on it—then that is a success! The group is policing themselves and sees things differently than you do!

Once you have provided feedback regarding the disruptive behavior and gained group or individual feedback on your observations, the next step is to help the group decide whether they want to change the group behavior and ground rules. Remember, your role as a facilitator is to guide the group toward successful decision making. An effective facilitator can maximize participation, productivity, and satisfaction and should focus on managing the decision-making process and supporting the group through the various stages of group development.

Managing disruptive behavior isn't easy! It's a challenge that is unique to each facilitator and each group. The key is to recognize the individual and group thought processes occurring and to select the appropriate response or time to intervene.

The phrase "managing conflict" may be a bit of a misnomer when facilitating meetings. Productive meetings don't necessarily quash conflicts—rather they provide an opportunity to air disagreements and express opinions. The dynamics and synergy result in large leaps forward and generate a plethora of ideas.

To reap the value of conflict, facilitators need to create an environment that allows participants to disagree publicly. In fact, the facilitator's role is to encourage and protect minority opinions. So how do facilitators walk a fine line to encourage conflict and opinions while avoiding destructive conflict? Consider these guidelines:

- ◆ look for shared goals and win–win situations
- ◆ clarify, sort, and value differences
- ◆ gain commitment to change attitudes and modes of communication when necessary
- ◆ openly praise group members who are willing to suggest new and different approaches

- analyze why conflicts keep occurring—usually participants aren't fighting about what they say they are fighting about
- encourage individuals to take the initiative to change personally
- model the kind of behavior that shows a comfort level with conflict.

When possible, encourage the use of "I" statements rather than "you" statements to depersonalize conflict. Using "I" statements means turning statements from accusations ("you did . . . ") into statements of fact or personal feeling ("I felt this way when this happened . . . "). Depersonalizing a conflict involves looking at a problem objectively.

The next chapter describes another important aspect of planning an effective facilitation session—creating the right climate—including setting up the room and adjusting physical environment factors.

STEP **7**

Create an Effective Climate

It's a common scenario: The meeting room is too hot, the lights are too dim, and the coffee is tepid. The facilitator is miles away, the slide projector does not focus, and the other group members are grumbling to one another in small groups about "a waste of time."

Believe it or not, but the details of where a meeting is held and how the room is set up may seem minor—but the fact is, these details affect the meeting's success. Rooms that are too small, uncomfortable, or not equipped properly serve as stumbling blocks to what otherwise might have been a very productive facilitation session.

STEP 8

Staging the Environment

The physical environment can have a major impact on the success of any meeting. No matter how well designed the facilitation plan, regardless of how talented you are as a facilitator, a good session in a poor environment might add up to a waste of time and money for everyone involved.

When selecting a room, be sure that the physical setting matches the facilitation session goals. Meetings can take place in an amazing range of rooms including theaters, storage rooms, classrooms, restaurants, and so on. Given the inevitable limitations that come along with the type of room assigned for the meeting, you must express your wants and needs, if you have a say in where and when the facilitation session takes places. When you are asked what you want and need—never say (or think), "Don't worry about me, any place is fine." Take advantage of the opportunity to have control over the room logistics and the ability to create a comfortable atmosphere to meet the session needs.

Setting Up the Room

The single factor that determines the success of any facilitation session is the seating. Placement of chairs—and possibly tables—can contribute immensely to facilitating open group communication and accomplishing objectives.

POINTER

Encourage quick stretch breaks if the group has been sitting for 60–90 minutes. These breaks are best timed when changing topics or when transitioning from a discussion to an activity.

Determining where group members will sit can influence the level of participation. Some seating arrangements make it difficult—if not impossible—to interrupt the facilitator. Other arrangements encourage participation of the entire group. So depending on how much you want to control the group, or get their direct involvement, use one of the seating arrangements described in this section.

There is no single way to set up a room for a facilitation session. Because some setups work better for certain kinds of meetings than others, be sure to state your preferences. Descriptions of each type of room setup follow. Table 8.1 lists the most common room setups, as well as when to use each.

Rounds

Some people also refer to this configuration as pods. Actually, the term "rounds" connotes the shape of the table used—when in reality the table shape might really be square or rectangular. In this configuration, the facilitator and any audiovisual equipment are usually at the front of the room. Although the number of people at each table will vary, table seating usually averages between four and 10 people depending on the number of tables and the size of the group. Rounds work well for groups of at least 15 people, especially when you want them to work in small groups. This setup creates a friendly environment with the flexibility to choose the best audiovisuals to support the meeting.

Setting up rounds requires a room large enough to allow ample space between the tables without chairs brushing up next to each other. The biggest challenge when using this setup is that some participants may need to crane their necks to see the facilitator or audiovisuals based on the position of their chairs.

Classroom Style

This is similar to traditional school classroom seating with rows of desks or tables and chairs all facing the facilitator, who is standing in front. This type of arrangement usually gives a formal tone with all eyes on the facilitator and does not allow for a great deal of movement or interaction among participants.

Most participants will be able to see easily both high- and low-tech visual aids including flipcharts, whiteboards, and presentation software or slides. If the room is very long or very wide, however, some group members may feel like they are in the remote recesses of the room and may have difficulty seeing any visuals. This setup is the least conducive to facilitating group discussions and interactivity.

TABLE 8.1
Room Setup Matrix

Style	When to Use	When Not to Use	Alternatives
Rounds	• Larger groups • Work in teams • Small-group interaction • When using audiovisuals	• Room too small • Group less than 15	• Classroom • Chevron
Classroom	• Any size group depending on room size • When using audiovisuals • When focus is on the presenter	• You want group interaction • Room dimensions are too long or wide	• Chevron • Rounds • U-shape
U-Shape	• Smaller group size • Open environment • When using audiovisuals	• Small room • Large group • Work in teams	• Classroom • Chevron • Conference
Chevron	• Large groups • For presenters who like to move • When using visuals	• When a warm, personal atmosphere is needed	• U-shape • Rounds • Classroom
Conference	• Small group • Group discussion • Formal and intimate	• Room to spread out • When using audiovisuals that require room • Presenter movement	• Classroom • U-shape
Theater	• Large group • Focus on presenter • When using audiovisuals	• Establish intimate environment • Small group • Group interaction	• Rounds • Classroom • Chevron

U-Shaped Configuration

This room configuration is often popular for group and workshop-type settings where all participants can see each other and the facilitator has plenty of room to walk around. This setup is particularly useful when you want to have groups of two or three people talk or work together.

This setup works best for groups of 12 to 24 people if the room is large enough. If the group is too big or too small, then the purpose of this room setup is defeated. Be careful not to cram too many tables and chairs into a room that is too small. This will make it difficult for participants to walk around the outside of the tables so they can leave the room when needed.

Chevron

This arrangement combines the best features of the classroom and rounds arrangements. Like the classroom setup, rows of tables are placed on angles and positioned behind each other. This forms the letter "V" with a main aisle in the middle. Like the rounds setup, it makes for easy pairing of groups already set at different tables.

This setup offers two main benefits. It can accommodate large groups and because the tables are angled, participants can easily maneuver and walk around the room. This setup also enables the facilitator to easily walk down the main aisle and to make a variety of visual aids visible to the group.

POINTER

Take note of signs of boredom, fatigue, or other indications of lack of involvement from the group. When you see these signals, try to quickly get to an activity, change the pace of the discussions, or perhaps switch participants to different subgroups to work on activities with peers to provide a different point of view.

STEP 8

One disadvantage is that the participants in the back of the room, even with the tables angled, might have difficulty seeing some of the visuals if the group is large. This type of setup also does not create a very warm or intimate setup as most of the participants are looking at the back sides of the people in front of them.

Conference Style

This style usually involves the group sitting in chairs around a large conference table. The facilitator can take a seat at the table, either at the head for a stronger presence or at any chair for a more informal effect. This type of arrangement works well for both formal and informal meetings in which the group is relatively small, depending on the size of the room.

Keep in mind that some participants might be a bit confined if they cannot walk around the table. This setup is also not as conducive to group activities as rounds or other setups.

Considering Other Room Elements

Facilitators need to keep room size and equipment requirements in mind when planning the meeting environment.

Screens

Another way to check the adequacy of dimensions of a room is to judge all distances from the width of the screen that will be used for visuals. Follow these guidelines:

◆ The distance from the screen to the last row of seats should not exceed six screen-widths.
◆ The distance to the front row of seats should be at least twice the width of the screen. Participants who are closer than that will experience discomfort and fatigue.
◆ The proper width of the viewing area is three screen-widths. No one should be more than one screen-width to the left or right of the screen.

- Ceiling height is important. The room's ceiling should be high enough—a minimum of nine feet—to permit people seated in the last row to see the bottom of the screen over, not around, the heads of those in front of them.
- Try to use screens that recede into the ceiling and that automatically raise and lower.

Audiovisual Setup

POINTER

Confirm that all participants can easily see and hear all meeting discussions and visuals. Beware of any posts or areas that obscure the participants' view or line of sight.

Chances are you'll be using at least one type of media to support the meeting and facilitation session flow. Although visuals can really enhance and clarify your issues and ideas, they can also turn the meeting into a disaster if you haven't appropriately planned and specified what you need in the meeting room. Prior to the facilitation session make sure you have accounted for the items listed below when using visual aids:

- Verify that there are enough outlets to accommodate all audiovisual equipment needs. Know the location of each and arrange to have any extension cords or power strips you will need.
- Tape down or cover any cords or wires that might pose tripping or electrical hazards.
- Familiarize yourself with each piece of equipment before the meeting and "cue up" any visuals.
- Prepare a contingency plan if any equipment malfunctions such as locating replacement bulbs, batteries, and so on.
- Identify the on-site audiovisual contact and how he/she can be reached should you need help.

Lecterns and Tables

A lectern is a small desk that usually sits on a podium or table where facilitators can rest their meeting and facilitation-plan

STEP 8

notes. Although lecterns often act like a security blanket for less-experienced facilitators (who want to be anchored to one place yet still appear experienced), be careful that they do not limit movement and facilitation of group processes and activities.

You might want to consider asking for an appropriately sized table to spread out notes, transparencies, handouts, props, or other meeting materials. If needed, arrange to have extra tables set up for handouts, and additional meeting materials.

Planning for the Group's Comfort

The session participants need to be comfortable to be effective. If they are distracted by heat or noise, for example, they will not be able to focus on the tasks at hand.

Temperature

Because room temperatures can vary wildly, ensure that both the participants and you will be comfortable. Prior to the meeting, be sure to find out how to control the room temperature. For example, can you adjust it yourself within the room or do you need to call someone within the building or at a remote location to request a temperature change? Here are some guidelines to consider:

◆ Set the thermostat for a comfortable level, depending on the season, size of the room, and the audience.

STEP 8

- It's probably best if the room is a little cool at the start of the presentation because the room will likely heat up as more people join the session and because some audiovisual equipment tends to throw off heat.
- Keep the room somewhat cooler if the audience is likely to be wearing business suits, which are often made of wool.
- For a daytime presentation in a room with windows, consider the effect of sunlight on the room temperature. Adjust the curtains or blinds—and perhaps the thermostat—accordingly.

Lighting

Lighting is an important factor in creating a comfortable environment for the audience. Not only does lighting affect the mood of the participants (prime sleepy time after lunch), but it is also a key factor in how well the audience can see visual aids and their ability to take notes.

Just as you need to know how to adjust the room temperature, lighting is no different. Be sure that you know how to dim and change the lighting. These are the lighting guidelines:

- Find out what lighting operations are available at the presentation site either by asking the sponsor or by visiting the site prior to presentation day.
- Locate the lighting controls for all lights in the room and practice using the dimmer and slide switches.
- Determine what settings you plan to use during various segments of the meeting. For example, if you are going to go through introductions or an opening activity, turn the lights up bright. Dim the lights when appropriate to enable the group to see the visual aids easily.
- If you cannot access the lighting controls easily during the meeting, arrange to have someone sit by the controls to make the changes for you.

STEP **8**

Noise Level

The noise level outside your room can affect the meeting—especially if you're located in a hotel or a noisy conference center.

If you are in a room separated from other rooms by a partition or near the kitchen entrance, check the noise level. If the noise is unacceptable, raise your concerns with the primary client contact or the facility contact to address the issue.

Food and Breaks

It's not unusual for continental breakfast items or snacks to be readily available in the meeting room or immediately outside the door. In fact, you might even be asked to conduct a facilitation session over lunchtime or at a dinner meeting. Because food service can affect the meeting—if you have any say in the matter, consider these things:

◆ Get to know the people who are handling the food service, and be clear about your expectations regarding the kinds of food that will be served, and when, how, and where the food will be set up.

◆ Opt for lighter, nutritious fare such as fruit or pasta salads and small sandwiches. Heavier food tends to make people drowsy, especially right after lunch or in late afternoon. Arrange for plenty of bottled water and juices as alternatives to sodas, as well as both decaffeinated and caffeinated coffee and tea.

◆ If possible, ask for the food service to be set up in advance so that it does not interfere with the meeting. If this is not possible, arrange for the food to be set up outside the meeting room to minimize the noise and disturbance.

Now that you have considered the various elements needed to create a comfortable, well-planned facilitation site, use Tool 8.1 to verify that the meeting room you will be using suits your needs.

With the room logistics out of the way, the next step in the process is to facilitate the meeting. The next chapter focuses on how to hone your skills to facilitate with a business focus.

STEP 8

TOOL 8.1

Facilitation-Site Checklist

To ensure the facilitation session location will promote interaction and support planned activities, follow these guidelines. Keep in mind that for longer meetings, comfortable chairs are essential.

Location

☐ Is the meeting room located away from high-traffic areas that might lead to interruptions?

☐ If necessary, are there signs directing participants to facilitation sessions, breakout rooms, break areas?

☐ Is there a system set up to minimize outside interruptions?

☐ Have all telephones been disconnected from inside the meeting room?

☐ Can you easily control the temperature and ventilation in the room?

Room Size and Shape

☐ Is the room the correct size for the type of facilitation session and activities that you are planning?

☐ Is the room free from any elements that will obstruct the view, such as columns?

☐ Is there enough room for audiovisual equipment?

☐ Is there enough clearance between tables and chairs?

☐ Are doorways wide enough for audiovisual equipment and disabled participants to easily pass through?

☐ If any breakout rooms are to be used, do they all have the equipment and supplies required, and are they in close proximity to the main meeting room?

☐ If you will be leaving the meeting room for a lunch break, can you secure the room to ensure that materials, laptops, or other valuable items are safe?

☐ What arrangements do you need to make if the meeting takes place over breaks or multiple days to ensure that cleaning crews do not throw out flipcharts, handouts, or other materials that might be on the walls and tables?

Walls and Ceilings

☐ Can the walls accommodate charts and panels?

☐ Are the ceilings high enough to accommodate projection screens?

☐ Do the walls contain enough electrical outlets? If computers are to be used, will antisurge electrical outlets be needed?

☐ Are light switches easily accessible?

☐ Can different parts of the room—for example, at the front of the room near the screen—receive different kinds of lighting?

Tool 8.1, continued

Noise Control

❒ Is the room too close to the street?
❒ Is the room near an alleyway or loading dock?
❒ Is the room located near building renovation or where heavy machinery is being used?
❒ Are elevators too near the room?
❒ Is a noisy session scheduled for the adjoining room?
❒ Is there a dividing wall that does not shut out noise from the adjacent room?

Furniture

❒ Do chairs have wheels that permit them to be moved without noise?
❒ Depending on the size of the group, are swivel chairs available?
❒ Do chairs have armrests that allow people to rest their arms at a 90-degree angle?
❒ Are there sufficient whiteboards or flipcharts, as well as markers?

Use of Technology

❒ Are there flexible cable outlets for computer hookups?
❒ Are there in-floor jacks?
❒ Are there electrical in-floor outlets at least every eight feet?
❒ Have you checked the audiovisual equipment?
❒ Will the facility have extra light bulbs and extension cords available or do you need to supply them?

STEP 8

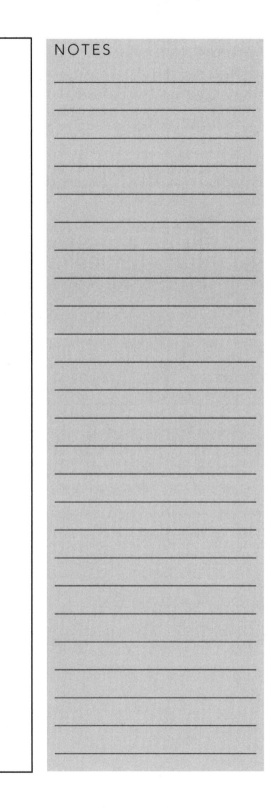

NOTES

Facilitate with a Business Focus

With all the meeting prep work out of the way, you're ready to facilitate. Being prepared makes all the difference in the world when it comes to facilitating an effective meeting. It also important to know how to start a facilitation session and to ensure that the discussion remains focused so defined outcomes will be accomplished.

Preparing the Room

Allow enough time before the participants arrive to get yourself and the room set up. As a best practice, consider these items:

- Check the seating arrangements. Are the chairs and tables the way you want them?
- Adjust the lighting.
- Check the audiovisual and computer equipment you plan to use. Be sure you know how to operate the equipment and that it's working properly.

STEP 9

Arrive at the meeting room early to check all equipment; arrange the furniture; set up your flipcharts, handouts, and so forth.

◆ Arrange visual aids—such as flipcharts for documenting the meeting, brainstorming, or other activities—so that everyone can see them.

◆ Check that you have allotted enough time on the agenda to cover all topics, have enough handouts for everyone, and that you have all materials needed for all planned activities, and so on.

◆ Display meeting objectives and the agenda. If you plan to have the participants define the session objectives and goals, post either blank flipcharts to facilitate the activity or post defined objectives for them to react to and refine.

Starting a Facilitation Session

A productive facilitation session does not necessarily begin once every invitee arrives; it begins at the time planned. Use this checklist to get you through the first few minutes of any facilitation session.

◆ **Do not stop and restart the meeting**—the participants arriving on time recognize that you are ready for them and that you don't intend to waste their time. This recognition helps to set the climate for a productive meeting.

◆ **Display enthusiasm**—be energetic and upbeat from the start and maintain your enthusiasm throughout the meeting.

◆ **Make sure everyone knows each other**—introduce any participants who are new to the group. Consider structured icebreakers for the initial kick-off meeting or facilitation session to help everyone introduce him or herself and learn more about the other participants.

- **Review the meeting objectives and agenda**—consider the professional level of the participants and the success of their past experiences working together, then determine whether it is necessary to review the group rules. If this is the first time the group is meeting, then solicit a list of ground rules from the group and display them during subsequent meetings.
- **Appoint a participant(s) for these key tasks such as** keeping track of time and recording meeting notes.

Keeping the Facilitation Session on Track

Effective facilitation sessions rely heavily on excellent use of facilitation techniques within the meeting in general and with individual activities. To keep the session and participants on task consider these tips:

- **Stick to the agenda**—the agenda is your roadmap to accomplishing the defined objectives. Follow it. Deviate only if you confirm with the group that a discussion is taking longer than planned—and then if the group decides to continue discussing the subject adjust the timetable as needed; if they decide to table the topic then stick to the agenda timing
- **Maintain a productive climate**—model the behavior that you expect participants to follow. Listen closely. Speak frankly. Encourage feedback and accept criticism professionally. Keep an open mind. Evaluate ideas, not people. Positively reinforce creative thinking. Do not dominate the meeting.

STEP **9**

- ◆ **Encourage and structure participation**—call on group members for input and ensure that only one person speaks at a time.
- ◆ **Ask good questions**—use a variety of questioning techniques, such as open-ended questions, to encourage participation and discussion. Avoid leading, personal, trick, or unanswerable questions.
- ◆ **Provide constructive feedback**—make sure feedback is useful and includes positive or neutral statements.
- ◆ **Give or get clarification of vague statements**—persist until the intended meaning is clear. Participants will otherwise interpret according to their individual experiences, sparking later disagreements and time-wasting backtracking to figure out what was meant.
- ◆ **Discourage generalizations**—ask participants who generalize or stereotype to evaluate the accuracy of their statements. Query these individuals for specific examples to help direct responses.
- ◆ **Protect minority opinions**—ensure that the least popular opinions get a full hearing and respect.
- ◆ **Keep participants on track**—intervene if any participants get off the subject for more than a few seconds. Make sure they don't use the facilitation session as a platform to vent personal frustrations about unrelated matters.
- ◆ **Reduce tensions**—intervene if conflicts between participants get out of hand and threaten to destroy meeting effectiveness. Do not deny or bury conflict, but try to help participants sort out their differences professionally.

- **Observe participants**—besides listening to participants, observe their behavior. Watch for signs of boredom, frustration, and other productivity reducers; then deal promptly with the problem. Energize the group with an activity or challenging questions; address causes of frustration, and so forth.

- **Provide necessary breaks**—don't wait for signs of restlessness by participants; call a short break once a meeting runs longer than 90 minutes.

- **Maintain professionalism and enthusiasm**—show interest in activities and display patience with participants throughout. Set an upbeat, productive example for participants whose energy may wane.

- **Put it in a parking lot**—discussions in meetings can raise a lot of issues, questions, and ideas that won't contribute to the purpose of the meeting, but are nonetheless valuable. To record such ideas, use a parking lot, which can take the form of a flipchart. When participants bring up useful ideas to explore at another time, tell them to put it in the parking lot. That way you will have a record of and can easily follow up on those ideas at another time. Individuals can also get unrelated concerns heard, "let go of any baggage," and return to focusing on the topic at hand.

- **Review periodically**—at appropriate points in the meeting, summarize and review what has been accomplished so far and clarify what remains to be done. This will help the group to stay on track for achieving the meeting objectives.

- **Maintain control of the meeting**—all these guidelines point to the major task of the facilitator: maintaining control of the facilitation session. It is your responsibility to ensure order and productivity so as to guide the group to achieve the stated outcomes.

STEP 9

Facilitation Tips

Successful facilitators use several techniques to create participation, to control the session, and to guide participants and discussions to achieve the stated objectives. Consider adding these techniques to your facilitation skills.

Tip	Explanation
Ask questions to gain participation	Ask open-ended questions that invite response, especially "what" and "how" questions. Close-ended questions stifle participation. Use close-ended questions only when you want to end discussion and move on.
Use transitions	Participants need to know when one topic has closed and another has begun. Transitions don't have to be fancy. A statement as simple as "Now that we have discussed X, let's move on to Y" works well.
Control discussions	Regardless of the participation level, you need to help the group work effectively and guide them during discussions to achieve objectives. That means that you need to remind the group of time. If a discussion is taking longer than planned, pose the options—for example, the group can continue with the discussion and remove something else from the agenda, or table the current discussion until another time. Intervene when needed to keep the discussion on track.
Remain neutral	If the group gets into a debate, clarify and summarize both sides and then move on. Don't express your own opinion (unless the debate concerns a factual matter) because participants with an opposing view may feel put down or that you are not being fair on a certain topic.
Don't wing it	Winging it carries some very big risks. You might go on time-consuming tangents, you might lead yourself into a discussion that is not appropriate, or you might steal your own thunder for a later subject.

Tip	Explanation
Affirm	Find something to reinforce and affirm in every comment. You can always affirm a person's effort at participation. When you treat people with respect, they will feel comfortable participating.
Watch and respond to body language	When you see furrowed brows and puzzled looks, ask the group if they understand. For example, you may say, "Some of you look a little puzzled. Is something not making sense?"
Don't be afraid of silence	Sometimes people are simply thinking and need a little time. When you ask a question, mentally count to 10 (slowly!) before rephrasing or redirecting the question.
Debrief thoroughly	Plan key questions that you will ask at the end of an activity or session to be sure that the participants are actively engaged—and as much as possible, come to consensus on topics or ideas. Do not ad-lib a debriefing session!

Using Reframing to Keep Discussion Going

Successful facilitators use reframing as a technique to encourage participants to understand one another's point of view. Rephrasing any judgmental or blaming comments and posing them back to the group helps to neutralize potentially charged comments and keeps the focus on the issues. This technique helps group members to hear each other in a neutral language so that they can continue to move forward with discussions and thereby accomplish objectives.

Keeping Groups on Track

Being on track in a meeting means that the group is progressing with the agenda and is moving toward accomplishing the agreed-upon goal(s). That doesn't mean that the group needs to strictly follow the agenda minute by minute. As a facilitator, you need to allow the group enough latitude for creative discussions, brainstorming, activities, and healthy disagreements as long as they are helping to achieve the stated outcomes. When trying to determine whether to let a discussion continue or if you need to redirect the group in another direction, consider these guidelines:

◆ Review the agenda and determine if the time constraints allow for more discussion or if you need to intervene.

◆ Review the ground rules regarding discussions that aren't relevant to the agenda and achieving the session objectives. If the discussion is relevant, but is throwing the agenda timing off, ask the group if they want to continue with the discussion (at the sacrifice of something else), or if the discussion should be tabled until another time to follow the agenda's timing.

◆ Assess why the group has gone off track. Confirm that the group members are clear about the session goals. For example, are participants focused on their own needs over the needs of the group (for example, airing their personal frustrations rather than focusing on the topic at hand)?

◆ Point out the agenda and remind the group of what needs to be accomplished and help them to understand the time requirements. If needed, bring them back to the appropriate step in the process. For example, if some people already have preconceived ideas without having gone through the entire process, intervene and ask them to hold off on making final decisions before having experienced the full session with the group.

- If one person is getting sidetracked, ask him or her to explain how his or her comments link to the topic or objectives to try to get the conversation back on track.
- Point out your unbiased observations—for example, by saying "I'm sensing that the group is having a bit of heart burn about the new pension plan." Try to uncover the core issue and get the group back on track with the topics and the agenda—or get the group to agree on what item(s) come off the agenda if more time is to be spent on the current topic.

Communicating Effectively

Everything that goes on in a facilitation session involves both verbal and nonverbal communication. The group shares ideas, listens, questions strategies, makes decisions, and may feel alienated from or part of the group based on the nonverbal communication of other group members. For example, if one chatty group member begins to speak and other participants instantly roll their eyes, this behavior sends a message loud and clear not only to the speaker but to other group members as well.

Experienced facilitators communicate effectively with groups using both verbal and nonverbal techniques and encourage this same behavior from the group participants.

Verbal Communication Skills

Verbal communication can immediately engage or turn off a group. Voice inflection is a key asset that enables facilitators to capture a group's attention and hold its interest. In any meeting, how you say something is just as important as what you are saying. To improve your verbal communication, consider sharpening these skills:

STEP 9

- **Projection**—the group has to be able to hear you and other participants in every part of the room. Depending on the acoustics in the meeting room, be prepared to ratchet up your voice projection and avoid inadvertently dropping the volume after the first few sentences of the meeting opening. As a best practice, repeat some comments or questions from meeting participants to ensure that all group members can hear and follow the dialog.

- **Pitch**—the dreaded monotone voice has lulled many a group participant to sleep. When facilitating, avoid droning on and never modulating the pitch of your voice up or down. Having a monotone delivery is usually the result of paying more attention to saying the exact words listed on the facilitator outline or agenda rather than listening to how you are saying the words. Let the group hear a change in your pitch when you are excited about something in the meeting or as a result of their discussions or activities. Modulate the pitch of your voice to accentuate more serious information. The group will take its cues not only from what you say, but sometimes even more important, how you say it.

- **Pronunciation**—if the group can't understand what you are saying, it's as if you didn't say it at all. Successful facilitators demonstrate exceptional diction—that is, the art of speaking precisely so that each word is clearly heard and understood to its fullest. Be sure to enunciate each word clearly when facilitating, using questioning techniques, or rephrasing. In certain parts of the country, slight dialects may be difficult to understand until listeners' ears get attuned to the sound and how specific words are pronounced. Keep this in mind if you have an accent or when facilitating meetings in certain areas of the country or abroad.

- **Pace**—good facilitators adjust their rate of speaking to accentuate a feeling or mood. Although the average rate of speech is about 140 words per minute, to show enthusiasm or energy for a particular point try increasing the amount of words accordingly. To make an important point perfectly clear or to emphasize something, try slowing down the rate to as few as 100 words per minute. This isn't science, so you don't have to get out a stopwatch and count. Rather, understand that you can create a mood and atmosphere for your meeting just by how you use your voice.

Pauses and Fillers

Pauses can add emphasis in just the right parts of any facilitated meeting. For example, a carefully placed pause can help to focus attention on a topic before you have a group work on an activity or before transitioning to a new topic. Pauses after you pose an idea or question also provide time for the group to think about what you're saying. By pausing and remaining silent, you encourage the group to share their thoughts or provide feedback.

Fillers—those words that creep into your speech to fill silence while you are thinking or transitioning to a new thought—include uhs, ums, ers, ahs, okay, right, and you know. Filler words are one of the fastest ways to annoy a group and even turn their focus to jotting down tick marks every time you use one. Don't be afraid to pause and leave silence between your sentences and thoughts. Skilled, confident facilitators are comfortable with silence and use it effectively to their advantage. Do not feel compelled to fill every silent moment with a filler word. Silence is an excellent facilitation tool to get the group to react to what was said and share opinions or ideas.

Nonverbal Communication Skills

Body language—meaning how you look and move—can enhance or undermine your facilitation skills. Based on different studies, it is usually accepted that between seven and 10 percent of the effectiveness of a meeting comes from the words the facilitator uses. Because the remaining 90 percent of meeting effectiveness is

STEP 9

attributed to nonverbal communication, facilitators need to be cognizant of their body language (and that of the group as well!) and use gestures, eye contact, and facial expressions to enhance communication and sharing of ideas.

STEP **9**

Body Language and Gestures

Many new facilitators struggle with exactly what they should be doing with their hands and bodies when guiding a group in a facilitation session. For example, should they lean on or grip the table for security? Rock or sway? Stand poker straight with hands at their sides? Cross their arms in front of their chests? The answer is—none of these!

Keep in mind that a facilitation session is about the participants. As such, the facilitator needs to sort of "disappear" into the background and let the group run with ideas and discussions. Because facilitators aren't invisible—they need to use body language and gestures effectively to help communication—to emphasize, show agreement, and maintain group interest. In general, use movement when you want to convey enthusiasm and energy about a particular point or result of an activity during the meeting. Seasoned facilitators walk to different parts of the room while making eye contact with the group members, especially if they are working in subgroups or on assigned activities. Movement can be used to engage all the group members, especially if you approach different areas of the room to make personal contact with the participants. This technique keeps everyone focused as you help to guide the group through a process for them to achieve the session goals.

Gestures refer to hand and body movements that are part of any meeting or form of communication. When you watch a play,

POINTER

Use effective gestures to help convey information and engage the participants' interest. This helps to show your enthusiasm about the meeting and interest in the group, and adds energy to the group. Your interest and enthusiasm are often contagious!

STEP 9

the actors use gestures to convey emotions, add emphasis to particular points, paint a mental picture, and so on. As such, consider these points regarding body language and gestures when facilitating a meeting:

- **Stance**—taking a natural stance but not looking too casual is important when facilitating a session. You want to project a comfortable, confident image but not look too casual. As a general rule, stand with legs about 18 inches apart or so (depending on your size), and equally distribute your weight on each foot, with your arms in a comfortable position at your sides or lightly resting on the table if you are seated.

- **Pay attention to and eliminate unconscious body language**—some gestures and movements can distract the group, such distractions include fidgeting, pacing, clicking a pen cap, and jingling keys or coins in pockets.

- **Use gestures for emphasis**—for example, if you say, "There are three steps in the new workflow process," then hold up three fingers sequentially as you articulate each point.

- **Observe the audience's body language**—facial expressions, down-turned eyes, looks of concern, fidgeting, or slouching are all signs of boredom, lack of interest, or lack of understanding.

- **Use positive facial expressions**—including smiles, expressive eyes, looks of concern, empathy, and encouragement. Look at your face in the mirror. How do you communicate feelings and emotions? How do you use your eyes, eyebrows, and mouth to express yourself?

- **Never sit behind a desk or stand behind a podium**—during your facilitation session. This establishes a barrier between you and the group. Put more life into the meeting by moving freely about the room. Facilitators who trap themselves behind the podium and venture out occasionally to write on a flipchart appear less than enthusiastic and confident.

- **Walk toward participants as they respond**—to your questions. This encourages them to continue. As a participant responds, nod your head slowly to show you hear what she or he is asking. If you need to think through what has been asked or to clarify the question, consider paraphrasing the question back or say, "so if I understand your question, you are asking . . . "

Above all, demonstrate enthusiasm and passion about the topic and the opportunity to facilitate. Your enthusiasm is contagious and often generates interest and positive feelings from the group.

Eye Contact and Facial Expressions

Making eye contact and exaggerating or animating facial expressions shows the group that you are engaging with them. So how much eye contact is appropriate? As a general rule, spend five or six seconds of eye contact at least once with each member of the group, making sure that you look at everyone when facilitating. Eye contact is also an opportunity for a facilitator to get a feel for how the group is reacting to the meeting, discussions, and other participants.

Following Up

With the meeting nearly at a close, what's a facilitator to do—pack up and leave? Not quite. In fact, the close of the meeting and follow-up on action items is mission-critical for the group to continue to make progress toward the goals outside of meeting hours. At the close of a meeting, don't forget to:

STEP 9

- Type up and distribute the notes from the meeting. Make sure that everyone who attended the meeting receives a copy as well as anyone affected by the outcomes of the meeting who did not attend.
- Plan to follow up on commitments. If you said that you were going to do something—make sure that you do it in a timely manner!
- Plan a follow-up meeting to make sure that commitments are being upheld and the purpose of the meeting is achieved. Follow-up meetings often point out if any new problems have surfaced that meeting participants need to solve.

You have now reviewed all the material necessary for preparing a masterful facilitation session. Tool 9.1 provides a handy checklist to use to verify that you have not overlooked any necessary elements prior to meeting day!

With the meeting nearly at a close, one last item is up for consideration—evaluation. The next chapter provides several evaluation techniques that you can employ to gather feedback and to continuously improve your facilitation skills.

TOOL 9.1

Countdown-to-Successful-Facilitation Checklist

Use this final-countdown checklist to help you relax and ensure that everything will go off without a hitch the day of the facilitation session.

2+ Weeks Before the Meeting (Start as Soon as Possible)

- ❒ Determine and confirm the purpose of the meeting, develop the session objectives and conduct an informal group analysis if you have not met the participants previously.
- ❒ Make the room arrangements, including equipment requests, supplies, refreshments, and so on.
- ❒ Create the meeting agenda, the facilitation session plan, and all visual aids.
- ❒ Select the type of facilitation techniques you want to use to create session interactivity.
- ❒ Develop the specific questions to ask the group and plan the activities to generate ideas, reach consensus, and achieve the session objectives.
- ❒ Make a list of all supporting meeting materials that you need (for example, handouts, worksheets, sticky notes, and so on).
- ❒ Do a run through and fine-tune the facilitation plan.

One Week Before the Facilitation Session

- ❒ Confirm that you have the right date and time of the meeting.
- ❒ Confirm that participants have received the meeting invitation.
- ❒ Confirm that the room and set-up arrangements you indicated will be ready for meeting day.
- ❒ Rehearse the facilitation session flow with a friendly critic and ask for feedback and ideas.
- ❒ Make any final adjustments to the facilitation plan.
- ❒ Memorize the opening of the facilitation session and how you plan to transition to other topics or activities during the meeting.
- ❒ Practice using all audiovisuals including practicing with flipcharts, switching to overhead transparencies or presentation software slides. Be sure to click through all of the slides to remember where any special effects such as dissolves, animation, or sounds occur in relation to your notes. Check for any misspellings.
- ❒ Pick out the clothes you plan to wear—remember, wear what you are going to be most comfortable in (preferably nothing new) that is slightly more formal than your audience's attire.
- ❒ If necessary, send presentation materials and any supplies ahead of time and call to be sure that they arrived.

(continued on next page)

STEP 9

Tool 9.1, continued

☐ Confirm the directions for the meeting location.
☐ Exchange phone numbers with the main contact person or sponsor of the meeting—especially if you are traveling quite a distance to the meeting location.
☐ Visualize what a successful facilitation session looks like in your mind's eye.

Meeting Day

☐ Arrive at least 30 minutes to 1 hour prior to the facilitation session time.
☐ Verify the meeting room location.
☐ Identify the on-site audiovisual contact or how to contact the meeting sponsor.
☐ Ask if any materials that you sent ahead of time have been delivered to the meeting room.
☐ Test all equipment.
☐ Tape down cords or power strips to prevent tripping hazards.
☐ Focus all equipment.
☐ Arrange your facilitation plan, notes, handouts, other session materials, tape, markers, and so on.
☐ Get a glass or bottle of water and paper towels.
☐ Scout out the restroom location.
☐ Arrange participants' handouts at their seats or on tables.
☐ Tidy up the room by hiding empty boxes, and so on.

Before You Begin the Facilitation Session

☐ Review the first 90 seconds of your opening.
☐ Do deep breathing and stretch techniques to help you relax.
☐ Run through your visualization and envision success and how you want the session to flow.
☐ Greet the participants.

Evaluate the Facilitation Session

OVERVIEW

Conducting a self-evaluation

Having the group critique itself

Having the group evaluate the facilitator

Having a trained observer conduct the evaluation

The last step in the process of creating and leading successful facilitation sessions is to evaluate what worked and what did not. Given the amount of time that people spend in meetings, isn't it surprising how seldom the effectiveness of a meeting is evaluated?

Keep in mind that the point of evaluating a facilitation session is to allow continuous improvement. The evaluation process can happen on several levels—for example, you may critique yourself, have the group critique itself, have the group provide feedback about your skills as a facilitator, and you may even have a trained observer attend the facilitation session with the sole purpose of providing you with expert feedback on how to improve your skills. Let's look at each evaluation option and some suggestions on how to gather the feedback.

Conducting a Self-Evaluation

After the meeting ends, you can reflect back on the meeting and how reality compared with what you planned. When conducting a

STEP **10**

self-evaluation, be careful to be objective and evaluate what happened from an outsider's perspective. The goal is improvement for future meetings! To facilitate this process, consider using the tool shown in Table 10.1.

Having the Group Critique Itself

One way to have a group learn from experience is by critiquing its own success during or at the conclusion of a meeting. For example, you can post a flipchart with one half labeled "What we did well" and the other half labeled "What we need to improve." Ask participants to reflect on the meeting and to help complete the flipchart. Many of these ideas may be incorporated info future meetings or may find themselves on a growing list of ground rules as the group figures out how to efficiently work together.

Having the Group Evaluate the Facilitator

The group members provide a wealth of evaluation information. Keep in mind that many of the facilitation session participants may not be objective when providing feedback during the evaluation process—but nonetheless, they are a valuable source information on how to improve future meetings.

TABLE 10.1

Self-Evaluation of a Meeting

A. Objectives

    1.   What were the meeting objectives?

    2.   Were they accomplished?

        ❒ Yes   ❒ No   ❒ Not Sure

    3.   Which objectives were not completely accomplished?

    4.   Why not? (Be specific.)

B. Time

    5.   Were objectives accomplished in minimum time?

        ❒ Yes   ❒ No   ❒ Not Sure

    6.   If objectives were not accomplished in minimum time, why not? (Be specific.)

C. Participants

    7.   In your opinion, how satisfied were participants with the meeting?

        ❒ Very Satisfied   ❒ Satisfied
        ❒ Dissatisfied   ❒ Very Dissatisfied

(continued on next page)

Table 10.1, continued

D.   If I were conducting the meeting again, what would I do the same? What would I do differently?

	Same	Different	Comments
Location			
Scheduled time			
Selection of participants			
Objectives			
Room setup			
Audiovisual aids			
Agenda			
My own preparation			
Advance notice to participants			
Introduction			
Amount of participation from the group			
Conclusion			

What else would I do differently?

Depending on the type of meeting, different types of forms might be most helpful to capture feedback anonymously. In general, consider using these guidelines to get honest, meaningful reactions to all types of meetings:

- Determine what kind of information you want (agenda topics, facilitation skills, room setup/facilities, handouts, visual aids, number and type of activities to engage the group and keep them involved, and so on).
- Prepare a written form to get reactions from the participants.
- Design the form so that the information can be tabulated and quantified. Do not use open-ended questions like: "How well did you like the program?" or "What did you like best?" These questions take too long to answer and are less meaningful.
- Allow participants to add comments that will help explain their reactions and offer suggestions for improvement. A good question is, "What would have made the meeting more effective?" or "How could the meeting have been improved?"
- Obtain honest reactions by removing any fear from repercussions for negative comments. The best way to do this is to make the forms anonymous and have participants put them on a table on their way out of the room.

Having a Trained Observer Conduct the Evaluation

Having a trained observer sit quietly in the back of the room and objectively observe the facilitation session can provide helpful evaluation information for improvement. Depending on the type of

Identify the type of information that you want to receive feedback on (for example, agenda topics, facilitation skills, room setup, visual aids, activities, and so on) and then craft the evaluation form to match the input you seek.

meeting, you might want the facilitator to focus on certain aspects of the session or your skills and jot down general notes on a pad of paper, or to gather more formal feedback, perhaps have the observer complete a form as observations are made during the session.

No matter which techniques are used, be receptive to comments from the trained observer. Don't be defensive—the trained observer's goal is to help you improve future meetings.

When having a trained observer evaluate your facilitation sessions, consider using a form similar to Table 10.2 to systematically gather formal feedback in specific areas.

No matter which evaluation techniques you decide to employ (the more the better!), some sort of evaluation should be conducted at the end of each facilitation session in an effort to capitalize on and maximize what went well and to diminish or eliminate the less-than-desirable occurrences. That's how skilled facilitators continue to hone and perfect their skills in specific areas to become truly successful facilitators.

TABLE 10.2
Evaluation by a Trained Observer

	Poor	Fair	Good	Very Good	Excellent
Statement of Objectives Comment:	❑	❑	❑	❑	❑
Presentation Effectiveness Comment:	❑	❑	❑	❑	❑
Ratio of Presentation to Participation Comment:	❑	❑	❑	❑	❑
Control of the Meeting Comment:	❑	❑	❑	❑	❑
Use of Visual Aids Comment:	❑	❑	❑	❑	❑
Effectiveness of Group Involvement Comment:	❑	❑	❑	❑	❑
Conclusion of Meeting Comment:	❑	❑	❑	❑	❑
Overall Effectiveness Comment:	❑	❑	❑	❑	❑

Suggestions for Improvement:

Physical Facilities	Poor	Fair	Good	Very Good	Excellent
• Room Setup	❑	❑	❑	❑	❑
• Temperature	❑	❑	❑	❑	❑
• Quiet	❑	❑	❑	❑	❑
• Comfort	❑	❑	❑	❑	❑
• Ventilation	❑	❑	❑	❑	❑

Introduction	Poor	Fair	Good	Very Good	Excellent
• Start on Time	❑	❑	❑	❑	❑
• Create Interest and Attention	❑	❑	❑	❑	❑
• Clarify Objectives	❑	❑	❑	❑	❑

(continued on next page)

STEP 10

Table 10.2, continued

	Poor	Fair	Good	Very Good	Excellent
Main Body					
• Information Clearly Presented	❏	❏	❏	❏	❏
• Ratio of Presentation to Discussion	❏	❏	❏	❏	❏
Audiovisual Aids					
• Selection	❏	❏	❏	❏	❏
• Use	❏	❏	❏	❏	❏
Other					
• Attitude of Facilitator Toward Group	❏	❏	❏	❏	❏
• Maintenance of Interest and Enthusiasm	❏	❏	❏	❏	❏
• Handling of People Problems (Tangents, Dominating Conversations, etc.)	❏	❏	❏	❏	❏
• Control of Meeting	❏	❏	❏	❏	❏
Conclusion					
• Summary of Meeting, Decisions, and Next Steps	❏	❏	❏	❏	❏
• Accomplishment of Objectives	❏	❏	❏	❏	❏
• Final Comments and Assignments	❏	❏	❏	❏	❏
• End Meeting on Time	❏	❏	❏	❏	❏

CONCLUSION:
DEVELOPING YOUR
SKILLS

Continuous learning is critical to the success of the individual, business unit, and the organization. An organization's only sustainable advantage is its human capital. How that human capital continually develops to address corporate and individual needs is a critical factor of success.

Beyond the scope of this book—to discuss 10 steps to creating and guiding effective facilitation sessions—is your role of continuing development. Your role as a facilitator should not stop at the meeting door. As a facilitator you influence groups and enable teams to work effectively and productively to accomplish a set of predefined goals and objectives.

To become an effective facilitator, work on honing your skills by strengthening your major weaknesses. Successful facilitators continually develop themselves by reading, attending seminars or workshops, tackling challenging job assignments, coaching, and so on. Use the following worksheet to continue to develop your skills in creating and leading productive meetings.

Instructions:

1. Describe one strength you want to hone, and one weakness you want to overcome.
2. Identify the method for development and required resources.
3. Establish a timeline for your development activities.
4. Determine the required feedback so that you can gauge the extent of your improvement.

Describe One Strength

Method for Development	Resources	Timeline	Feedback

Describe One Weakness

Method for Development	Resources	Timeline	Feedback

BIBLIOGRAPHY

Bedrosian, M. (reprinted 1995). "How to Make a Large Group Presentation." *Infoline* No. 259102. Alexandria, VA: ASTD Press.

Biech, E., M. Danahy, and B. Drake. (reprinted 1993). "Diagnostic Tools for Quality Control." *Infoline* No. 259109. Alexandria, VA: ASTD Press.

Callahan, M., and C. Russo, eds. (1999). "10 Great Games and How to Use Them." *Infoline* No. 258411. Alexandria, VA: ASTD Press.

Cassidy, Michael. (1999). "Group Decision Making." *Infoline* No. 259906. Alexandria, VA: ASTD Press.

Darraugh, Barbara. (reprinted 2000). "How to Facilitate." *Infoline* No. 259406. Alexandria, VA: ASTD Press.

———. (reprinted 1997). "Group Process Tools." *Infoline* No. 259407. Alexandria, VA: ASTD Press.

Eline, L. (revised 1997). "How to Prepare and Use Effective Visual Aids." *Infoline* No. 258410. Alexandria, VA: ASTD Press.

Estep, T. (2005). "Meetings that Work!" *Infoline* No. 250505. Alexandria, VA: ASTD Press.

Finkel, C., and A. Finkel. (revised 2000). "Facilities Planning." *Infoline* No. 258504. Alexandria, VA: ASTD Press.

Jacobson, S. (1994). "Neurolinguistic Programming." *Infoline* No. 259404. Alexandria, VA: ASTD Press.

Kirkpatrick, Donald. (2006). *How to Conduct Productive Meetings*. Alexandria, VA: ASTD Press.

Kirrane, D. (1988). "Be a Better Speaker." *Infoline* No. 258802. Alexandria, VA: ASTD Press.

McCain, D., and D. Tobey. (2004). *Facilitation Basics*. Alexandria, VA: ASTD Press.

Merriam-Webster's Collegiate Dictionary (11th ed.). (2005). Springfield, MA: Merriam-Webster.

Piskurich, G. (2002). *HPI Essentials*. Alexandria, VA: ASTD Press.

Prezioso, R. (revised 1999). "Icebreakers." *Infoline* No. 258911. Alexandria, VA: ASTD Press.

Rosania, R.J. (2003). *Presentation Basics*. Alexandria, VA: ASTD Press.

Rose, C. (1987) *Accelerated Learning*. New York: Bantam Dell.

Russo, C.S. (2000). "Storytelling." *Infoline* No. 250006. Alexandria, VA: ASTD Press.

Spruell, G. (revised 1997). "More Productive Meetings." *Infoline* No. 258710. Alexandria, VA: ASTD Press.

Tuckman, B., and M.A. Jensen. (1997). "Stages of Small Group Development Revisited." *Group and Organizational Studies*, 4, 419–427.

Wircenski, J. and R. Sullivan. (1986). "Make Every Presentation a Winner." *Infoline* No. 258606. Alexandria, VA: ASTD Press.

I N D E X

environmental style, 138
facilitation-site checklist, 146–47
food, 144–45
lecterns, 141–42
lighting, 143
noise level, 143–44
room setup matrix, 138
rounds, 137–38
screens, 140–41
setup, 136–40
tables, 141–42
temperature, 142–43
theater, 138
U-shape configuration, 138–39
Evaluation of facilitation session, 49,
167–74
group evaluation of facilitator, 168–71
group self-critique, 168
self-evaluation, 167–70
trained observer, evaluation by, 171–74
Evaluator learning style, 103–4, 106
External environmental factors, 68
Eye contact, 163

Facial expressions, 162–63
Facilitation, 7–16
acceptance of others, by facilitator, 11
audience profile, creation of, 12–14
conflict resolution, as facilitator skill, 11
defined, 7–8
differentiating facilitators from
presenters, 9–10
empathy of facilitator, 11
leading skills, 11
listening skills, 11
managing process, 10
neutrality of facilitator, 11
participants, focus on, 8
participative style, 11
presenter, facilitator, distinguished, 8–10
problem solving, 11
questioning, 11
resource, facilitator as, 11
roles of facilitator, 10–11
self-assessment role inventory, 15–16
sharing, 11
skills of facilitator, 11–12
Facilitation plan, 17–30
agenda preparation, 26–30
appropriateness of meeting,
determination of, 19–20
business goals, identification of, 18–19
facilitator role, 23–24
needs of client, understanding, 17–18
note-takers, 24
participant selection, 20–25
planning sessions, 25–26
timekeepers, 23
Facilitation techniques, 39–48
Facilitator role, 23–24
Facilitator tools, 58–76
Fearfulness of new technology, 92–93
Feedback, 128–34, 152
Fillers, 159

Fish bone diagramming, 64–67
Five-why technique, 68–69
Flipcharts, 83–86
advantages of using, 85–86
creation of, 84–85
touch, turn, talk method, 83
when to avoid using, 86
Focus, in differentiation of presenters,
facilitators, 9
Follow up, 163–64
Food, 144–45
Force field analyses, 74–76
Formal presentations, 91, 93
Forming, team development stage, 115

Generalizations, discouraging, 152
Gestures, 161–63
Getting acquainted, 33
Graphs, 47
Griper, 131
Ground rules for session, 37–38
Group appropriateness, 77–78
Group conflict, 113–34
acting stupid, 125
active listening, 119
attentive listening, 119
behaviors enhancing, hindering group
effectiveness, 118–19
body language, use of, 125
breaks, suggesting, 125
bungler, 130
common threads, searching for, 125
conversationalist, 129
debriefing group, 125
describing behavior, 128–34
diagnosing, 126–28
disruptive behaviors, 129–31
feedback, 128–34
griper, 131
group management of process, 125
heckler, 129
intervention, 122–28
listening skills, 118–19
maintenance behavior, 123–24
maintenance functions, 122
managing, 126–28
meaning, interpreting from behaviors,
119
mule, 131
observation, 118–19
participation, encouraging, 125
passive listening, 119
personal attacks, discouraging, 125
personality problems, 130
process obstacles, describing, 125
quiet participant, 130
rambler, 129
ready answer, 129
specificity, 126
strategies for dealing with, 113–14
straw man, presentation of, 125
summarizing, 125
talker, 131
task function, 119, 123–24

THE **_ASTD_** MISSION:

Through exceptional learning and performance, we create a world that works better.

The American Society for Training & Development provides world-class professional development opportunities, content, networking, and resources for workplace learning and performance professionals.

Dedicated to helping members increase their relevance, enhance their skills, and align learning to business results, ASTD sets the standard for best practices within the profession.

The society is recognized for shaping global discussions on workforce development and providing the tools to demonstrate the impact of learning on the organizational bottom line. ASTD represents the profession's interests to corporate executives, policy makers, academic leaders, small business owners, and consultants through world-class content, convening opportunities, professional development, and awards and recognition.

Resources
- *T+D (Training + Development)* Magazine
- ASTD Press
- Industry Newsletters
- Research and Benchmarking
- Representation to Policy Makers

Networking
- Local Chapters
- Online Communities
- ASTD Connect
- Benchmarking Forum
- Learning Executives Network

Professional Development
- Certificate Programs
- Conferences and Workshops
- Online Learning
- CPLP™ Certification Through the ASTD Certification Institute
- Career Center and Job Bank

Awards and Best Practices
- ASTD BEST Awards
- Excellence in Practice Awards
- E-Learning Courseware Certification (ECC) Through the ASTD Certification Institute

Learn more about ASTD at www.astd.org.
1.800.628.2783 (U.S.) or 1.703.683.8100
customercare@astd.org

090735.62220